iii
third eye

an imprint of Skywriter Books

SKYWRITER

FIGHTING FIRE

Caroline Paul

First published by St. Martin's Press, New York, NY, May 1998

Published in the United States by Third Eye, an imprint of Skywriter Books, Sausalito, California
www.skywriterbooks.com

Skywriter Books and Third Eye are registered trademarks of One Pink Hat Corp.

LIBRARY OF CONGRESS CATALOGING-IN-PUBLICATION DATA

Library of Congress Cataloging-in-Publication Data

Paul, Caroline.
Fighting Fire/ by Caroline Paul.
p. cm.
ISBN 978-0-9822797-3-1
1. Paul, Caroline. 2. Women firefighters—California-San Francisco—Biography
3. San Francisco (Calif.). Fire dept.—officials and employees—Biography
I. Title
TH9118.P38A3 1998
363.37'092'279461-dc21
[B]
98-9791

Cover design by Julie Munsayac; interior design by Stuart Silberman

For more information, please contact the publisher at
Skywriter Books, PO Box 2630, Sausalito, CA 94966
info@skywriterbooks.com

To the members of the San Francisco Fire Department
Brave, always.

and

Eric Martin
Adventurer
Writer
Friend

INTRODUCTION

The fifth alarm at the Delta Hotel was the biggest fire of my career. It was the whole shebang: a huge, five-story residential hotel; people hanging out the windows, screaming; a hundred residents spilling out the exits; the two top floors aflame.

Unfortunately it happened after I'd finished writing *Fighting Fire* in 1997. And it wasn't the only rip-roaring incident that missed inclusion in the original publication. I was a firefighter before, during, and after the book. The adventures kept coming, and each one seemed bigger and badder than the last.

This is one reason I've decided to re-edit and re-issue *Fighting Fire*.

The second reason is that I'm a better writer. Who doesn't want to improve upon the past? Faced with my younger self, of course I wanted to inspect her narrative decisions. I could sternly scrutinize that first time writer: cut repetition, smooth awkward sentences, and pull back on raw, earnest, wide-eyed prose.

On the other hand, I'm well aware that was who I was back then — raw, earnest, wide-eyed. I was coming from the heart. Perhaps I should leave the book be.

A memoir is an accounting of the life you've experienced. As long as the facts remain, what's wrong with re-editing? But a memoir is also a reflection of who you are at the time of writing. If I now rewrote what I had written then, what would that mean for the book? I was peering backwards at myself from a new vantage point, 15 years or more hence. Would it be the same book? Could I fiddle with some of the words, but keep the essence?

I decided that I could.

So you hold a revised version of *Fighting Fire*. I've cut a few initial chapters. I've added a few incidents. However, I didn't add as many as I thought. Yes, there were so many more adventures, but why transcribe them unless they illuminate something about my journey? So the Delta Hotel fire was scrapped because it went something like this: Big fire! People hanging out windows! Crawling in the dark!

You'd read that before.

Also not mentioned: the injury that eventually retired me. I fell in a fire, badly bruising bone and chipping cartilage in my knee. A year and many fires later, I finally agreed to surgery. I eventually had a total of four surgeries, and after retirement, a replaced knee.

After thirteen and a half years with the San Francisco Fire Department, I left quietly, and in shock. I was ashamed of being injured, and it was too early to be done. I fell into one of those depressions where your hair gets greasy and you lose weight, and you don't speak much, and what you do say is really boring. It was terrible. If I wasn't a firefighter, who was I?

Luckily the very things whose loss I felt so deeply were also now a part of me. With the stubbornness and resolve I'd learned on the job, and with a firefighter's unique understanding that life is just too short, I shook myself free of depression after a year and a half. I became a full time writer, working out of the Writer's Grotto, an office space and distinguished literary community here in San Francisco. In my fellow writers, I've found a new fire crew, and I'm journeying through another rewarding career. Writers aren't the most adventurous bunch, so it's not the same as a day on Rescue 2, of course. But writing and firefighting have this in common: both ask that you face yourself, your true self, every day.

I hope you enjoy this updated edition.

Caroline Paul,
July 2011

PREFACE

It always begins the same way.

First the fire coat, one arm at a time. It is snapped—usually only three of the snaps—and clipped. From here the fingers slide upwards to the collar, feeling the rough Nomex cloth and the hard, chipped paint of the name that lines the back of it. Then the belt is cinched tight, the buckle jingling against the small crash axe, which is spun to a precise place against the right thigh where it will not tangle with the air pack. Thick leather gloves, often stiff with ash, are put on, and each hand is flexed, one, two, three times to loosen them.

Finally, there is the fire helmet. It is picked up in one quick motion with the palm outstretched. Fingers crook around the front shield—mine says RESCUE 2—and lift it to eye level. Then the head is bent, as if in prayer, and some sweep a hand across the hair to smooth it down. I do. I push back my bangs in one quick movement. Then I lean the leather against my forehead. Finally, the head is brought up and the helmet slid back, simultaneously. Most of the men leave the chinstraps to dangle, but I cinch mine up with one quick pull. The helmet has yet to fit well over my array of bobby pins and hair ties.

Today is no exception. Despite the chaos as we race to the incident—the siren is at full wail and the air horn blasts angrily at each street intersection—I have re-enacted these small, precise movements. My crew has done the same. Alberto is the one exception—as the rest of us jump quickly out of the rig, which has pulled to an abrupt and bumpy stop on the sidewalk, he stops and drops his helmet from above as if it was any other old hat, and wriggles it from side to side to snare it onto his head. Then he starts a careful, deliberate walk.

We head toward a crowd that has gathered in a large fragmented half circle. I smell the smoke before I see it; sour and acrid, it conjures up false images of fireplaces and marshmallows. Then I see it, heavy and dark gray, pumping out of two side windows and spewing towards the midday sky. Over the sound of burning wood—a belching, crackling roar—I hear the collective gasp of the crowd.

Two engines are already parked in the busy intersection ahead. Flames now leap from the upper windows. Even on the sidewalk, it has grown hot. Momentarily my crew and I stare, mesmerized like the onlookers. Above me, the fire reaches out into the day. In front of me, burning wood drops into the stairwell. For a millisecond, there is nothing but this power and beauty.

Another window blows out from the force of the heat. My throat tightens. My heart pounds. Not from fear, but from something else. Wonder. Awe. And a little bit of disbelief. There is something about fire that touches my soul. I know it's the same with the rest of my crew; fire moves us in a profound, primal way. In the face of it, we want to ask the bigger questions, the whys of existence. Lofty inappropriate questions like *why am I here on this earth?* and smaller ones like *how did I get here, to this place of being a firefighter?*

My lieutenant brushes by me. All our small rituals of certainty—coat buttoned, helmet on, air pack tight—are over. Now come the vast possibilities, the meeting of chance, fate and luck with skill and choice. Now comes the unknown of fire. There is no time for existential philosophy; I follow him into the roaring building.

1.

It is June 1986, and I am graduating from Stanford University. I should be happy, and I am, but I am also terrified. Unlike many of my peers, who have well planned trajectories of doctor, lawyer, banker, I have no idea what I want to do with my life. I only know that a desk job seems like prison and a corner office like solitary confinement. Mounds of paperwork? Long hours on a phone? No, thank you.

They call Stanford University "The Farm". No one minds; we like the romantic, hardworking, close-to-the-land ethic of the nickname, but otherwise we are not here to be farmers. We are here to take the world by storm, ascend to the tippy-top of the career ladder and then, once there, do some unexplained good for the world. Or so each graduation speech says. Meaningless, overused words like "spirit", "enthusiasm" and "potential" float toward us, and soon, bored, jittery, we stop listening.

It is a scalding spring day. I glance around, ridiculous in my black robe and sash, wishing that I had taped a funny message to my graduation hat like the people in front of me. *In debt. Thanks, mom. I need a job.* My friends are beside me—Rick, Sophia, Steve—and my family somewhere above.

I imagine the four of them in their folding chairs, trying to find me in the row of black hats below them. My twin will be sitting on the edge of her seat and her long neck will be angled forward as if listening; I know this without seeing her. I am less sure about my brother; he will drape himself over the metal frame, letting his hands dangle behind him, or he will be hunched over his knees with one finger playing with the chip on his front tooth. I made that chip myself a long time ago, during a particularly vicious Water Pic fight, back when Water Pics were in fashion and my brother and I used to fight, so I notice it often, with a soft, guilty feeling in my stomach.

My father has flown in from Massachusetts, my mother from Connecticut. Divorced for ten years, my parents speak politely to each other, but most of the time they convey messages in an orbital fashion— they do not speak towards, but around each other. *Your father is taking us out to dinner*, my mother says; the inference that my father does not exist in relation to her, only in relation to the kids, is clear. They slide away from us alternately, like buoys off shore, first my mother and then, as she drifts back, my father, in a seeming effort to avoid each other. Sometimes we wish that our parents did not both come to these events. But neither of them would have missed this day, when finally one of us graduates from college.

Alexandra walks up and hugs me.

"Hey, Mugsy," she says, using a code name from a secret club we had when we were kids.

"Hey, Black Jack," I say back.

We are identical twins, born six weeks early to surprised parents who had not prepared for two. It was a 12-hour labor, during which time my father gamely read the business section of the New York Times aloud to distract my mother; then she was wheeled into the delivery room and Alexandra slid out after a shot of Demerol and a whiff of oxygen. One of the doctors abruptly turned to a nurse and said, "My gosh, I think there's another one," and two minutes later I appeared, hairless, rat-like, with a purplish hue. "It was the most exciting moment of my life," my mother says of the experience. "That, and skydiving." At just over four pounds each, we were promptly put into incubators. My parents were too stunned to think of another name, so we were both labeled Baby A and Baby B, and sent home after two weeks.

My graduation gown entangles with Alexandra's slim arms as we hug, and I let my cap fall because I pretend that I do not care how I look, or that any of this matters so much. Friends offer high fives as they pass with their own families; "Can you believe it?" "Wow." "Woohooo!" Then my brother Jonathan lopes up and pulls both Alexandra and I into an enthusiastic embrace. "Now you've done it, smarty pants," he says to me, and grins.

All three of us were expected to earn a college degree, but my twin turned Stanford down four years ago in order to pursue an acting career, and my brother, full of street smarts, never liked school at all. He struggled, took the GED, passed, and vowed never to set foot in a classroom again. So it's just me. I'm not much of a school person either, so today my parents, both phi beta kappa (my mother from Trinity college, my father from Yale) are not only proud, but visibly relieved.

I will miss this place. Stanford University is beautiful, with elegant Spanish-style roofs and quaint Victorian houses. There are long pillared corridors and quadrangles with square stones that make just the right echo—a serious, concise tapping that narrows and ends in a delicate point of sound that lingers long after you have stepped there. I have made good friends, and together we have struggled through these college years with something like grace. However, the grace came easy; we struggled because we realized that college is a time of struggle and we played it like the script that it was. There was a sense that even the angst of youth was a routine expected of us. Now the script has ended. I want a new one to replace it, but that will have to wait, for now, at least, because I hear my father call out and wave his new video camera, bought especially for the occasion. "Can you three do that again?" he says, pushing us back together with a sweep of his hand, bringing the camera to eye level, squinting through it.

My father is someone who has always had a plan. Even when he worked on the General Motors assembly line in the summer during Harvard Business school with eighty seconds to assemble and screw on the radio antennae, he had vision, assessing how the plant could run better, putting ideas in the suggestions box until the foreman told him to quit it or he'd get fired. Eighty seconds, not only for the antennae, but to put two screws in the front door on one side and then run around the back end, lift the tire out, spray the upholstery with glue, reload the tire and press the carpet down. If you fumbled there was no time to correct your mistake. He said that workers ate lunch in the back of the cars and sometimes there were wrappers or banana peels left there, but eighty seconds was not enough time to clean it out, so the detritus was upholstered right into the car. My dad was born in the depression and carries with him a deep sense that honesty and efficiency are almost the same ethic, so when he tells this story he laughs, but there is an offended edge to it.

My father applied to the international banking firm of Morgan Stanley in his last year of business school. In the interview, he explained that nightmarish summer job at General Motors. Coincidentally, Morgan Stanley was a major investor in General Motors. My father assessed the assembly plant for the interviewers. The president of GM received a three-page letter, while my father was promptly hired to Morgan Stanley at a salary of $5,000 a year.

My dad's new video camera has a telescoping lens, auto-focus, and even sound. I am touched because I know that he does not like new-fangled, mechanical devices; now he fumbles with the buttons and forgets to take the lens cap off. For a moment it is hard to imagine my father outside of his awkward love for us: that he worked on forty-five cars an hour, loose screws, crooked upholstery and all; that he retired as a partner from a major investment banking firm; that he owns a farm and puts in his own fence-posts. That for all the best laid plans, he never expected twins. That he certainly never expected this, looking at his grown children so similar to each other in looks and bearing, wedged within the frame of his camera, but on their way to different lives. Now we stand absolutely still, smiles frozen on our faces for the camera, until my father remembers there is audio included. "Speech!" he calls out, and my brother says congratulations, congratulations to the only college graduate of this Paul generation.

2.

It's 4.30 in the morning, and I have the whole radio station to myself at this hour. The news is due at 7 AM, at which time I will put on my headset, slide behind the mike and read the stories I have compiled. Until then I will rush around like a dervish, coffee in one hand, various wire stories, newspapers and tape in the other.

Does journalism suit me? Not really. But I'm casting about desperately, trying to find something that I can settle on. To that end, I am part of KPFA's internship program, and it's great in its way, not at all like other internships, where you serve pastries and monitor copy machines and file papers alphabetically until you think you're going to faint. Here you are quickly trained, then given a tape recorder and a story to investigate, and thrown out into the world.

I have a paying gig too—right now I'm an editorial assistant at an important local legal paper. It's supposed to be a sweet job, a stepping stone to bigger things, but I can't see the value of articles about promotions, new court appointments and meager scandals. I'm bored to tears. I make surreptitious phone calls to friends, and wear unprofessional outfits. I should be fired. I *want* to be fired. Right now my future feels like a mundane flipbook where I sit behind a desk and move only my typing fingers, and it scares me.

My friends seem to be well on their way—Steve is a graphic designer, Sophia is in public policy school, Rick is an engineer, Scott is in law school. My brother cleans rugs and plans animal rights activities. My twin has just costarred in her first feature film, and there's talk of a television series. And me? I'm aimless. It's embarrassing just how aimless, the hours taking on a gelatinous quality, until I'm on the verge of what can only be depression, though at the time I don't know this, and think morosely that this is just life, gray, uncertain, monotonous.

The KPFA hallway is dark, so I switch on lights, head to the newsroom. Once there I turn the radio on to the national news, spread out the four newspapers I will scan, then bounce over to the teletype and tear off the long scroll of paper that has unfurled all over the floor. "Ripping wire," as they call it, is my favorite, because I read news as it happens. The teletype whirs, taps, and screeches, and stories filed by wire services like AP and Reuters gush forth in a white-papered torrent: toppled dictators, fatal bus crashes, celebrity arrests, dangerous toys just pulled from the market. I skim each story, tear off what I want, drop the rest at my feet. Then I wade frantically through the room, preparing the broadcast.

This morning there is another story about the San Francisco Fire Department. "Doctored Photo," it says, "New Racial Trouble." I scan it: a black man is erased from a photo that ran in the San Francisco Firefighter's Local 798 newsletter. The Union says it is because he is the only non-member; he is also the only black man and he belongs to the opposing Black Firefighters Association.

I remember other incidents in the recent past: Interracial fistfights in stations, a swastika near the desk of minority officers, lawsuits involving racial discrimination, the first class of women coming into the department under duress. I am fuzzy on the details, the exact accusations and counter accusations. But I write a snappy story on this latest scandal. I won't lead with it, I decide, but I'll put it near the top. It's distasteful in all the right ways, and will hold people's attention into minute three.

A few days later, at my gym, a wide shouldered man stops in front of me at the lat pull-down machine.

"You're strong," he says, crossing his arms and nodding thoughtfully. Taken aback, I shrug, and wait for him to move on. When he doesn't I say, "Okay, thanks," without much enthusiasm, so he'll take the hint that I'm not interested in talking when I work out.

But still he does not move, just keeps nodding and smiling. If he asks me on a date, I think, I will have to break it to him that I'm only interested in girls, which is true. It's a tossup whether this is the best strategy to shake the guy loose, however, as this information often piques a suitor's interest. Before I can decide on how to proceed, he breaks in.

"The San Francisco Fire Department is recruiting women," he says. "How about applying?"

I stare at him, a little aghast.

"The racist, sexist San Francisco Fire Department?" I say. "Thanks, but no."

The firefighter isn't phased. He grins cheerfully and says, "I hope you'll consider it anyway." He offers me an application card. "And, hey, don't always believe what the media says."

Since right now I *am* the media, this sentence immediately strikes home. After all, I don't research my data. As a beleaguered morning anchor at a listener sponsored station who handles the morning's stories by herself, I simply rip wire, or look at other people's reporting. My job is to catch the attention of the post-sleep, pre-coffee crowd—to simplify and to inflate.

I reach out, and take the application card.

"Okay," I say. "Why not?"

The man shakes my hand, and walks away.

Later, I twist the card through my fingers. It becomes damp, gray and funnel shaped. I have no intention of becoming a firefighter. Still, maybe I should go see for myself what this department is up to.

An undercover story for KPFA. Why not? Judging from the media stories I've already seen, this place is a hotbed of creeps and chauvinist pigs. What would it be like to fill out the application and go through the testing process? I could catch the department deep in their messy institutionalized racism and sexism. I could turn the experience into an exposé.

The more I think about this, the more it seems like a pretty good idea.

Finally, I smooth out the application card and fill it out. A few days later, I drop it into the mailbox.

3.

The Moscone Center is a huge mid-town complex designed for trade shows and conventions. I arrive in the early morning fog to take the test that begins the San Francisco Fire Department's entrance procedure. I am unprepared for the huge line that winds around the building and spreads out haphazardly near the front doors. Approximately 5,000 people had signed up for the test, and 3,159 have arrived to actually take it.

I can't carry in anything so there's no way to take notes, but I make observations to write down later. There aren't many women, for one. There are white men, of course. There are some blacks and Hispanics, more Asians. Who will get in? Who won't? Why do people want this job? It's all a mystery to me, but I don't ask questions. Instead I wait like the others, quiet, somber, contemplative. When it's time, I allow myself to be gently pulled in through the big glass doors by the polite, nervous sway of strangers.

The test is a curious one. In the video portion, firefighters assemble a piece of machinery. They are different ethnicities; one is a woman. The narrator speaks slowly, so slowly that snickers erupt from around the auditorium. Mid-snicker the video stops and the narrator asks a question (slowly, carefully) about the assemblage we have just seen. I realize that this test is trying to rid itself of all cultural, ethnic, class or gender biases. In addition, my tires aren't slashed, no firefighters grope me, there are no sexist slurs tossed my way. By the end of the day, I'm at a loss. There are no explosive truths here. There are no grim themes of exclusion and bigotry.

Momentarily I think that maybe there's a different story I can pursue, one where a large institution tries to right itself from past wrongs. But of course this isn't interesting news. I've been in the business long enough to know that this angle will be quickly shoved aside for sex scandals, shootouts, and shady multinationals invading developing countries. There is no undercover story here, at least not one that is controversial, and so I quickly forget about the San Francisco Fire Department. I do not see the firefighter in the gym again, and no new stories about the department pass over my KPFA desk. Alexandra asks about my mission a few days later. "No story," I tell her regretfully. I don't mention the test to my father, because an allusion to anything "undercover" would worry him. Nor to my mother; we don't speak much, and it seems unnecessary to update her on my life. She doesn't know my girlfriend, my current job, the newest of my roommates. When we do speak, it's only small talk, and the whole time I clutch the phone awkwardly to my ear and wish for it to be over, until we finally both mumble goodbye.

Mothers and daughters—it's always a prickly relationship. But ours is worse than just prickly, unfortunately. It is also cold and distant, and when that distance is bridged, angry. Why? There's never one reason, of course. But it seemed to begin on the day my mother picked up Gail Sheehy's *Passages*. Halfway through the book my mother went berserk. Or at least that's how it looked through the eyes of a teenager. She went back to school. She filed for divorce. She started dating a handsome young boyfriend. Mostly, she no longer cried unexpectedly in corners anymore, as she had for years; we wanted the disheveled, weepy mother we were used to, not this new, narrow-eyed, whirlwind. She explained that she was finally happy. Happy? From the vantage point of a fourteen year old, it was clear she had instead been brainwashed by aliens. For years after, my mother and I rarely talked, and when we did it was a short exchange, full of angry subtext and long silences. Now I am more polite and more adept at being distant, so our sentences are longer, but we have not reconciled. It's not all her fault, of course, and somewhere in the back of my young and immature mind I know this. But I don't admit it, precisely because I'm young and immature. And so it goes, strained conversation that leads to trepidation about future strained conversation, until ultimately it seems best not to speak at all.

One day, a month or so after the test, the phone rings and a man who identifies himself as a lieutenant asks to speak to me. "Yes," I stammer, confused.

"You've scored well on the fire exam for San Francisco," he says. He goes on to say that I qualify, along with 250 others, to go on to the next phase of testing: the physical agility test.

"What!" I say.

"What?" the lieutenant responds.

"I mean, okay. Wow. I passed." My brain is sluggish with shock. "Thanks for calling." I almost hang up, but the lieutenant interrupts.

"Yeah, Miss. But we need to confirm that you can go to your physical test appointment."

I always do unexceptionally on tests; there is no reason that this test should have been any different. Unless this was not just a good test score, but a portent. It's gotten to that point in my life; I'm looking for signs to guide me, instead of common sense. I must have been silent for a long time because finally the lieutenant, sounding irritated, says,

"We need your answer, Miss."

"Uh, well, I guess, okay.

"I need a yes or a no, miss."

A long pause.

"Yes."

I hang up, dazed. I walk down the stairs, hoping to run into a roommate. Then I walk back up and phone my twin.

"That's perfect for you," she says, upon hearing the news. Is she right? The truth is that we don't really understand what firefighters do.

"Well, they run into burning buildings," my twin says.

"I can do that," I say, and we both know that this at least is probably true. Certainly, I'm no stranger to dangerous situations. I'm a private pilot. I'm a paraglider. I'm a whitewater rafting guide. During college I took time off to train in the obscure sport of luge, which consists of an ice track and great speeds, and—in my case—lots of crashes and a hospital visit. In sum, I don't know much about firefighting, but I do know that I process adrenalin well.

"Come on, this is supposed to be a radio story. I should just stop."

"No, no, definitely not. What's the harm, Mugsy? Maybe something will happen. And if it doesn't, things will just go back to the way they are."

Which, of course, is what I'm afraid of.

4.

San Francisco's first recorded fire was a grass fire. This grass fire spread into the western part of the city in 1847. The population of two hundred quickly recognized the threat to these dry, windy hills and the first fire law went into effect: anyone setting alight brush or garbage would be fined five dollars.

This is the first hint of San Francisco's incendiary past; two years later San Francisco suffered six big fires (called the Great Fires). It was 1849, and gold had been found to the east; the city's population had skyrocketed to 25,000 people. For the next 18 months these Great Fires devastated the city, tearing through the huts and temporary houses erected by gold seekers. The fires had a strange effect: instead of cowering under the assault, San Franciscans rebuilt their homes within weeks of each razing. Each time the city emerged more beautiful and sturdier than before. Temporary wood and cotton paper houses became permanent brick structures as people who came west seeking their fortune fell in love with San Francisco.

Fire took on a mystical side: citizens boasted how many times they had been burnt out of their homes (four or five times was not uncommon), as if fire defined their character. Meanwhile, street preachers claimed that fire was "divine vengeance" wreaked on the rough, pagan drinkers and gamblers of this frontier town. Later, the official Seal of San Francisco became a phoenix rising from flames in front of the Golden Gate Bridge.

By the third Great Fire, however, the citizens began to think of forming a fire department. Benjamin Franklin had organized the first volunteers more than a half-century earlier, and all over America, brigades were springing up. And so, on October 1, 1850, the San Francisco Fire Department was born.

How could I ever be a firefighter? The first firefighter looked so little like me; he was as mythical as the fires he fought. Documents claimed that "to be a fireman was to be a gentleman," but there are numerous accounts of brawls breaking out between fire engine crews. Upon arrival at a fire, one engine company would routinely detach the hose of another engine company from the hydrant and substitute its own, and companies like Knickerbocker #5 and Monumental #6 were said to have shot at each other. At night crews did not work together but instead would creep furtively up to the fire and then at an opportune moment, race past rival crews, hauling their hand-pumped engine. Fights would break out by the hydrant, sometimes only broken up by the Chief of Police. These first firefighters were rough frontier men. They *were* fire, unpredictable, with flaming tempers and a capacity for both destruction and re-growth. It was volatile forces like these, as much as the later contributions of architects, politicians, and earnest citizens, that make San Francisco the beautiful city it is today.

But few of us are aware of it. On the surface, there is nothing that hints at San Francisco's charred, chaotic past. When we think of violent, temperamental forces in San Francisco, we think of earthquakes, with their monster-like capacity to open up and swallow us whole. But in 1906, the real damage came not from the famous earthquake, but from the fire afterwards. It lasted three days and devoured 28,000 buildings (twenty of them were firehouses). Today a hydrant on the spot where firefighters made their final, successful stand is painted gold and remains at Twentieth and Church Streets, a small reminder of the inferno.

To me, everything about San Francisco feels serene, and it's hard to imagine that the dirty, ashen hand of a firefighter shaped any of this. Bounded on three sides by water and bridges, our city feels like a splendid castle surrounded by a moat, insulated and separate. The hills undulate softly; the wheels of its cable cars hum quietly; its amiable surf rustles gently. Old Victorian houses are painted in lively colors; the one I live in is orange with yellow trim around the windows and the turret. Entranced by its own exotic beauty, San Francisco calls itself Baghdad-by-the-Bay, and in more snobbish moments simply The City, as if none other exists. It is no surprise, then, that San Franciscans know little about their fire department, and when that department is accused of "institutional racism and sexism" many are able to distance themselves. They forget that this is a town born from ashes and forged by flame, and that the predicaments of the fire department mirror the predicaments of the city.

Meanwhile, these hills are a perfect place to train for the physical part of the fire department's test. I rowed crew in college—a sport where men and women alike proudly showed off their blood blisters, where vomiting during practice was considered a badge of honor, and where everyone trained extra on the side, "for fun"—so I take to this workout with fervor. I have little idea what a firefighter does, but I have been briefed on the test, so I clumsily try to tailor my routine accordingly, mostly by carrying a backpack full of weights to simulate the "hose carry" event, where I must, among other things, carry a 60-lb hose bundle up four flights of stairs. Dogs bark and people stare as I take the neighborhood steps two at a time, then one at a time, and finally, near the top, in a slow-motion, lactic acid-induced stagger. Then I bend over my knees, catch my breath, and walk back down, to do it all over again.

Practice sessions for the test are held in a huge cement space said to be fire academy grounds, but which looks instead like a prison yard.

Also on these grounds is an active firehouse, and it is here that I first catch a glimpse of on-duty firefighters. They stand at a distance, leaning against the brick wall of their station, arms crossed, legs wide, their blue uniforms making them indistinct. We ignore them, but we know that they are there and cast furtive glances their way, intimidated, a little in awe.

It is 1988, and there are six women already in the department. They came in, under controversy, two years ago. I have not met them, but at the test practices we whisper about them sometimes, wondering how it would be to have been one of the first. There is a secret relief that we are not treading a completely new path, that there is a slight trail through the thicket for us. "Slight" is an overstatement: there are six women out of 1500 men. The trail is barely visible.

A few days later the firefighters are gone. Someone higher-up has told them that they cannot watch the test proceedings.

The practice sessions give me a chance to go through the phases of the actual test. First, I pull up on a rope with a weight on the end. I have no idea what this has to do with the job, but I am assured that it is pertinent. I lift a ladder. I drag a hose towards a white line. At the white line I drop the hose. Then I pick up a hose bundle, lug it up four long flights of stairs, drop it, and drag an eighty-pound person across the floor. It is not really a person, but an under-stuffed, hairless, overused dummy whose arms have been grabbed by so many of us that they are in imminent danger of falling off. Then I push a large pole up and down for a minute. I push against seventy-five pounds on the up-stroke and pull ninety-five pounds on the down-stroke. I start to hear the sound—a loud, rhythmic clanging—in my sleep.

I pass the test easily.

Then my acceptance to a graduate school film program arrives in the mail. Instead of elation, I feel as if something large and ominous has just walked into my path.

The two separate worlds of firefighting and film school offer an odd symmetry, anvil-shaped, as if to make a place on which to hammer my indecision into some definable form. At once I see the perfect crossroads in a heretofore jumbled lifestyle. Documentary filmmaking represents my East coast, WASP background. Here lies responsibility, social status and intellect. On the firefighting side of the anvil hangs something darker, more primal. It represents impulsiveness, rebellion and instinct—the part of me that flies planes, rafts rivers, climbs onto steep slippery roofs to look at stars. But this part of me has never been taken too seriously. Certainly it's not something I should base my life on. Right?

I shake my head; there is no crossroads, despite my lively imagination; being a firefighter is out of the question. I am on my way to film school in the fall. I send in my acceptance.

I go through with the last phase of the fire department's entrance procedure. I don't know why. I tell myself I don't like to quit, I like to see things through, why not finish it? But part of me knows that something more than momentum pulls me. I take a medical exam. Then I submit the information required for my background check: proof of residency, motor vehicles record, and police reports.

I have three speeding tickets and a long rap sheet, which I pull out crumpled from my bag. The investigating officer, a square-jawed firefighter with narrow, unsmiling eyes, smooths it out. He stares at the long list of misdemeanors.

"All, uh, protests," I say. He reads in silence.

"America, freedom of speech, and all that." I wonder whether I should explain: even my mother has been arrested for protesting nuclear weapons. We are not hippies, I want to say; my father still thinks Nixon should have stayed in office. We are simply Americans, standing up for what we believe, in the polite but firm manner encouraged by our forefathers. But I remain quiet. The man, scowling, finally says, "We can't disqualify for misdemeanors," clearly wishing that he could. He picks up my driving record, then shakes the paper in the air. "And slow down, Miss," he says, before jerking his chin forward once, and just like that, the interview is over.

Well, I think as I walk out, that's it. I blew it for myself. I'm off that list, for sure, once and for all. Oh, well, no big deal, I don't want this job, right? But I have a sinking sense of loss combined with the dull relief of someone who is pointed onto a flat, wide highway.

A few days later I am accepted to the San Francisco Fire Department Academy Class Number 75, off the first list under the 1988 United States federal court consent decree.

5.

Now, therefore it is hereby ordered, adjudged and decreed the federal court proclaims. With these words begins the "consent decree," the formal plan in place for the next seven years designed to combat the systemic racism and sexism of the San Francisco Fire Department.

I am part of this plan.

If I choose to be, at least. Instead, I panic. Me, a firefighter? My life has opened up many options for me, but it has almost completely closed off this one.

And the thought of telling my father scares me silly. For years he has paid for the finest of schools, and now I am contemplating a job where only a GED is required. This is not what he had in mind.

"Firefighting seems cool," says my brother, Jonathan. We sit on the front stairwell of the place where I live, while he smokes a cigarette. "But what about all that paramilitary bullshit?"

"I know," I say, remembering the first distinct image I had of a firefighter, from a photograph I saw in high school; in it, a crowd of black protesters scatters under the force of a fire hose held by a sharp-faced white man in uniform. My brother nods, remembering the photo too. But I know he is already entranced with the idea that his sister might be a firefighter. Yes, on the one hand there is this paramilitary bullshit; for a long-haired, lefty, vegan radical like my brother, that's a big concern. But on the other hand, there's the fire truck. Like most males, my brother spent a fair share of his childhood ramming matchbox cars together to produce fantastic accidents and then hovering matchbook rescue helicopters over the gruesome scene. He built Lego houses and recited all the ways they had burst into flame and then pushed the toy fire apparatus across the carpet while chirping siren sounds. The toys have long ago been put away, but the fascination has not, and now there's that gleam in his eye I recognize, that most men have when firefighting comes up in conversation, where large red trucks and large red engines take hold of their imagination and don't let go.

"Anyway, I'm in film school," I say, talking to myself more than anything.

My brother shrugs.

"I could do both, but... It just seems so, I don't know, *unlikely.*"

"Yeah."

I shake my head, exasperated at him. "Can you give me some advice, please?"

"All right," he says, and pauses. Then he explains that I mustn't care what my Stanford friends might think, nor what society says I should do as a woman. It's my life, and I should try this firefighting route, even if it means stepping into a racist, sexist quagmire, because he and I are both unconventional at heart, and unconventional people break the bonds of their past, and do things despite what the culture may say. I'm clearly qualified, he tells me, given my risk-full background and my physical fitness, so why don't I go in there and kick some fire dude ass. And while I'm at it, I get to swing an axe, handle a chainsaw, and drive a big red fire truck, and who could ask for more?

He doesn't quite say it this way, but this is what I know he means.

Then he adds, after a long pause, "Just don't tell Dad," and looks at me sheepishly.

✻ ✻ ✻

It is hard to know exactly what Dad will say, because Dad at once conforms to and dislikes his background. Why should he mind if I shuck mine, in favor of—let's admit it—a blue-collar job?

We are a family that has not drawn a genealogical tree, nor would ever want to. Our ancestors do not interest us much, and there are no claims to famous or infamous bloodlines. My mother comes from England, but gave up her passport with relief and became an American citizen. She shed everything British except her accent. My father talks little about the small town that he grew up in. He told me once that he had never heard of Yale University before he went there; he only knew that it was the farthest from Middletown, Ohio on his college list. Yet now, in Massachusetts, he still leads the reserved life of a Midwesterner. His only connection to a past is one not his own: my father collects antiques of every shape and size. He has a faded document from Leopold of Prussia which he has partly deciphered, a large 17th century clock that stands like a sentinel at his dining room door, and a pair of shelves so delicate that he points closely but never touches them. He understands the imprints on silver and the mint letters on coins. It is hard to figure him out or fit him neatly into any category. He is a man of high integrity, a peculiar product of what he has worked hard to forget and what he has worked hard to become. My parents are both at war with their past; as a result, the whole family is under the American illusion that we can constantly remake ourselves.

Firefighter: the word sticks to my lips, the syllables clumsy and strange. I can't possibly tell my father: he'll have a heart attack, a stroke, a fainting spell.

Alexandra points out that my father is in perfect health; it is I who looks pale and sweaty. She has just finished the film *Dragnet*, where in one scene she tackles a snake in a wide pit of water while in a wedding dress. The snake was fake but the pit of water and the wedding dress were real and she had to do take after take after take after take, so I believe that she knows about adversity.

"What should I do?" I ask her.

"You should do what makes you happy," she says.

I tell her that this Hallmark card advice is not helping. But in fact her tacit acceptance of whatever I decide gives me strength to take action.

Even if that action is to stall.

I call the San Francisco Fire Department. I ask if instead of accepting or refusing the position, can I put off the decision a little longer? "Okay, you're deferring," the brusque man on the other end says and pauses, while I imagine him scratching my name off of some formal piece of paper. "You are now deferred," he repeats and the phone goes dead.

When the "Quake of '89" strikes, I am on the top of the student union, on a break from one of my graduate school courses. The building is a gray stone monolith made to look modern and architecturally daring by its strange angles and concrete hummocks. I sit on a chair in a balcony-like area, on top of one of the concrete protrusions, when the earth moves angrily. My coffee, which is on the ground next to me, topples over; I cannot stand up for the shaking. Then I hear a collective moan from the campus and see students stream wildly out of buildings below me, like insects from under a rock that has just been kicked away. Inside the buildings, bookshelves have toppled, chairs have skittered sideways, and the lights have gone out.

Later, I watch the Marina neighborhood burn from a hilltop not far from my house. My housemates and I sit with our chins on our knees contemplating the strange orange haze.

The next day and for days afterwards the newspapers are full of the destruction and chaos. A freeway overpass has collapsed, and the Bay Bridge has lost a section to the tremors, closing it, so I must take the train across the bay to KPFA. Since the trains don't start early enough,

I leave the night before with a sleeping bag in hand and sleep in the office in order to get the news out on time.

As I scan the morning papers to collect my stories, I see a strange transformation. The San Francisco firefighters are now heroes. The Firefighter Who Wouldn't Give Up, reads a headline, detailing how one Firefighter Shannon crawled into a building to help a trapped woman. The building was leaking gas, and it was in imminent danger of collapse or fire. But he got to her, the account says, and reached for her hand. He promised that he would not leave without her. He cut her free with a chainsaw while the building burned.

Later he said, "When someone holds your hand and you are a few feet away... I couldn't go no matter what was happening."

Another San Francisco firefighter crawls into the sprawling debris of the Nimitz freeway, with no certainty that it would not collapse further and sandwich him. Seventy people and their Fords, Toyotas, and Hyundais are crushed or dying. Three other firefighters pull a man from the remains of an apartment; two minutes later the burning building falls.

I stare at the printed stories. Life is complex, I think, and these are complex men. Men who, despite their alleged racism or sexism, also reach in and hold hands with strangers at the risk of their own lives.

I pick up the phone.

"I'll take the job," I say to the man on the other end of the line.

6.

The San Francisco Fire Academy takes place in a series of makeshift plywood buildings erected for temporary use years ago and, like many things deemed temporary, remains still unchanged. The buildings are so flimsy that they shake when we enter, 30 new recruits wearing big work boots, filing by the stern looking lieutenants charged with our new education. The rooms are dark and stuffy and once seated on hard folding chairs, we shift and twist through long, tedious lectures.

Today the lieutenant draws a big triangle on the board.

"This is fire," he says sternly.

"Oxygen, fuel, heat." He points slowly to each corner of his drawing. "These elements are required for a flame."

"But the three elements must combine precisely. Too little oxygen," he says, "and there will be no fire, despite the dry wood and the hot match. Too little heat and the perfect fuel in the perfect oxygenated environment will not burn. The elements are all there, constantly, but they must be in the right proportions. It is a delicate dance."

We're hardly listening now. We yawn, disappointed. We don't want *Fire* to be a delicate dance. We want raging anger, the fight of a mythical beast. We want the legendary force with which Prometheus changed humankind. We want a wild creature, but we're getting something closer to pussycats.

"And there is a fourth element, a chemical reaction," the lieutenant continues, oblivious. He taps in the middle of the triangle and looks back at us blandly.

"That's a square," someone says, to snickering and shuffles.

When I told my father of my decision, finally, he paused to absorb this strange information. His daughter, a firefighter. "That's fine, honey," he said, but I could hear puzzlement in his voice. *Just a phase,* I imagined him thinking, as he added it to the list of other things that he has been simultaneously proud of and worried about: rafter, pilot, paraglider. "Just be careful. I have enough gray hairs as it is."

In the academy we are given a shiny yellow helmet, blue overalls, and a number. Quickly we are indistinguishable; woman, man, black, white, Asian, Hispanic, American Indian becoming blue-ish shapes bobbing nervously past hose lines and forcible entry tools, answering only to a numeral that is written everywhere—on our helmet, our books, our desk, our locker, and the place where we stand at line-up and salute. *Stand straighter, 27! You're up, 27! 27, next room, on the double.*

Training at the San Francisco Fire Academy takes fourteen weeks. From 7:30 a.m. to 5:30 p.m. we attend lectures and then go out to the asphalt-covered "yard" and simulate fire scenes. We learn to couple and uncouple hoses, name extinguishers and their specific uses, and recognize tools like the Chicago Door Opener and the ten-pound mall. We learn to "throw" ladders, the most menacing of which is the 50-foot ladder. While most ladders require two people, or sometimes three, to raise, "The Fifty" needs six. It weighs three hundred and fifty pounds, and at any given time in the raise, as few as two people may hold all the weight.

The only problem I seem to have is with my hair, which is long, and cut with bangs that fall over my eyes. *Hair!* Lt. Gibson barks at me, his southern accent clipped and stern. I've never been yelled at like this and I can't tell if he's pretending or he's really angry, but it doesn't matter; I have to fix my hair. In the mornings, the other women help me braid it, but every morning he warns me again. An ex-military man, he speaks in short bursts.

"Hair, 27," he says. "Don't meet regulations."

I nod silently, and try again the next day and eventually I figure it out, much to everyone's relief in my class, and perhaps Gibson's too.

My number falls between #26, quiet Tom Ellis on my left, and #28 Mark Fields on my right. #28 is part of a family legacy of San Francisco firefighters. Accordingly, he has a large, round physique and a vigorous blonde moustache; he looks like the quintessential firefighter. #26 is a stocky man of mixed heritage that is hard to pinpoint. He doesn't say much; what he does say is carefully thought out and reliable.

All day the lieutenants like to pontificate and rant; they chastise us loudly, and later we see them laughing in a corner, surely exchanging tales about how stupid we are. There are rules that seem to make no sense except as psychological conditioning: we are shown videos of explosions, of firefighters on fire, of melting apparatuses; we must always have a hose spanner in our pockets, despite the fact that we seldom use it; we must run when we cross the grounds, no exceptions.

The severest psychological test comes when we are told we must scale a seven-story building using thin ladders called "pompiers." These are fourteen-feet-long pieces of wood with small handles that run up either side; they resemble the vertebrae of some fragile, long dead creature. At the top is a long metal piece with small teeth, which grip the wooden sill of the window above. Pompiers were once carried on fire trucks to climb to windows normal ladders could not reach, but they are no longer in the field because they were deemed too dangerous. Instead, the academy uses them to test the mettle of recruits.

I start on the first floor and lean way out with the pompier in my hands. I flip its thin jaw to the window above. When it catches, I grip the threadlike frame tight, and climb. It sways and bends mercilessly;

I can hear the sill creak and groan. None of us can figure out how the pompier holds, and at some point, we are sure, one of the window frames will simply give way. But we do it anyway, crawling up the side of the building, swearing under our breath. At the sixth floor, we are told to belt ourselves to the ladder. Then comes the command: lean back. Way back. Arms out, crucifix-like. More. People hesitate, sweat, close their eyes, pray. Some let go briefly, only to be yelled at and told to do it again by the lieutenants below. One man throws up afterwards, claiming he has the flu. To me, it feels as glorious as flying.

I like all my classmates. They are smart and funny and hardworking and everyone seems to wish the best for the other. Still, it's a group and like most groups it quickly divides into quiet cliques. Lines are drawn depending on which high school one went to, what sports were played, who has family in the department. In other words, we drift toward those most similar to us. There are six of us women. Nothing direct has been said to us, but we all know that we are under scrutiny by our male classmates and our lieutenants. So we gravitate together, watching each other's backs, feeling loyalty.

Wendy is a paramedic and Anne is on her way to being a nurse; they help the rest of us with the Emergency Medical Technician tests. Together, we trade tips on the ladder throws, quiz each other in preparation for the weekly test, offer general encouragement. Jackie is the only black woman. She likes all of us, but as the herd of recruits subtly begins to fall into groups, Jackie makes it clear that she regards herself as black first, and then as a woman. She believes that is the way the world regards her. Being black in a white man's world is harder than being a woman in a white man's world, she says.

Unlike Jackie, I am not used to being in the minority. As a white, I have taken my inclusion for granted. As a Paul, my popularity has come easily. Only as a woman have I time and again understood what it feels like to be excluded. But when it happened (and it did), it seemed like a game. Mostly, I ignored it. Now, I no longer could.

❊ ❊ ❊

Firefighting itself is a new and different culture. For a woman, it's like being in a foreign country, with a big language barrier and strange customs. I have many male friends, but sadly this does not help me as much as I thought it would. The world I'm now in is about men, not men and women.

The social codes remain murky for me while the weeks in the academy slip by, but the job of a firefighter becomes clearer. To my surprise, we're not here just to fight fires. Our work involves anything from lockouts, to leaking roofs, to stuck elevators. But more often than anything, we are sent on medical calls.

Medical calls are fast becoming the most common emergencies that San Francisco firefighters respond to. This is a city guarded by 41 fire stations, judiciously placed so each is about three minutes from any destination in their area. But there are at most only 14 ambulances on the streets at any one time, and at night this can drop to seven. Sometimes an ambulance does not pull up to the scene for twenty minutes. Until then, it is the firefighter's job to keep the patient alive.

As a result, Emergency Medical Technician (EMT) training has come to the academy. We learn to use defibrillators and do cardiopulmonary resuscitation (CPR). We groan through slide shows of gross disfigurations and massive burns. We are taught to recognize a diabetic reaction, the last stages of labor, entry wounds, exit wounds, cerebral spinal fluid, and brain matter, and by the end, our skills land us somewhere in the vicinity of war medics and emergency room nurses.

When graduation finally rolls around, I still have more questions than answers about this new life. What *is* fire? All I have gotten so far is a triangle on a board, photos on a screen, some instruction on fire behavior.

But I am beginning to understand something else. The fire academy, under the blunt tutelage of the federal courts, has become a testing ground of another kind, where the social problems of a nation will now face off. Here we are, 30 people from different backgrounds, brought together in the fervent hope that we can not only work together, but that we can live together, and even bond. And why not? The fire department is an institution that knows how to battle great dangers. It is a place where courage and loyalty and teamwork is stressed. If there is anywhere that the difficulties of sexism and racism can be overcome, perhaps it really is the firehouse. Certainly a firefighter understands that under one circumstance we will come together: fighting fire.

Will I be a good firefighter? *Big fire, grab the big hose line,* my academy friend Ritch says, shrugging. *Little fire, little line. That's all we need to remember.* It is graduation day and I do not wear a gown this time, but a stiffly pressed uniform with a cap. My father arrives from Massachusetts; my mother does not come. Alexandra puts on my cap and we stand in front of a fire engine while Dad takes the obligatory picture. "Good going, Mugsy," she whispers.

7.

Station 53 stands on the edge of San Francisco's warehouse district. Here, the buildings squat like old, tired barns. Tar spots stain the streets. There are few cars, and remnants of train tracks cut haphazardly across sidewalks, ruins of a past age. On corners, hulls of buildings sag near cranes and bulldozers; the deep guttural sounds of destruction and reconstruction blend indistinguishably. It is a part of town neglected until recently, now gradually being patched by new buildings and streetlights.

I pull my bag out of the car and stand staring at the open station doors. In the bag are the trappings of my new life: fire helmet, fire coat, turnout pants (called "bunkers" in some fire departments, presumably because you tumble from your bunk and put them on). A sleeping bag. Toothpaste, toothbrush, hairbrush. A handful of bobby pins. Shower slippers. Tampons. Extra blue t-shirts, like the one I wear under my wool uniform shirt. I take out my coat and helmet, gaze at it all, then put the bag back into the car. I will come back for it later. I want to enter my first firehouse looking casual and self-assured, not staggering under a load of toiletries and bed accessories.

The firehouse doors are open, and the fire engine and the fire truck (Station 53 is a "double house"; a single house has only an engine) face me, nose out, the shiny chrome momentarily intimidating. Suddenly my legs are heavy, and my heart speeds up. I stare at the rigs, at the fire coats dropped around the floor, at the open locker doors. *Just walk in,* I tell myself. *No sense in standing here. Just walk in.*

Finally I start to move. The sunlight of the morning abruptly drops away as I step from the sidewalk into the station. The shadows adjust and I am inside. I take a deep breath. It smells like a fire station should, of ash and of something sharp, a mixture of diesel, wet leather and metal.

Just then a firefighter appears from behind the truck, his shirt untucked, an unlit cigar clamped between his teeth. He is short and trim and intent on something in his hand, which turns out to be a match. When he sees me, he stops.

"So you're the new girl." He does not remove the cigar when he speaks, just steadies it as if it is a nail to be hammered.

He nods at me, and his thin gray hair, hanging in slabs on his forehead, swings with the motion. I introduce myself and he turns to his left and leans in, squinting. "Speak up. I'm deaf, like the rest of these Jakeys," he says. "The sirens. You got to wear your ear protection, okay, or you'll end up like me." He laughs, understanding a new irony: in some ways I will never be like him, in other ways I will.

"I'm Tom," he says, sticking out his hand now. "Let me help you with your stuff." His face freezes then, and he withdraws his hand quickly. There have been specific instructions about how to act, what to say, what not to say. So now he adds, "Um, ya know, I'd do it for a guy."

"Thank you," I say, and walk back to my car for my bag. Relief floods Tom's face. He swings it on his shoulder and we walk into the firehouse.

A truck and an engine face me. Tom tells me to put my helmet and coat on the seat of my new assignment, the truck. I open a door, step on the running board, and drop my equipment inside. My new life has officially begun.

"Firefighter Paul," says a man, coming toward me. He has wide shoulders and the long lope of someone used to bending over to get under doorways. At 6'7" he is clearly not a man to be trifled with. "I'm your officer. Jim Leahy."

Captain Jim Leahy, to be precise. I have of course been given his name, but now I trip all over myself. "Hello. Captain, Captain Leahy," I stammer, walking his way, extending a hand.

"Jim," he says. "Call me Jim."

Tom shuffles off to light his cigar; Captain Leahy leads me to the kitchen. I follow him shyly. A dizziness washes over me. I have felt this vertigo before, on the first day of the academy.

You won't fit in. You are not a fireman.

Not that I know what a fireman is like. Fire Man, Jakey, Smoke-eater. There are many names. Fireman is no longer accurate for the new department, though it fits the old-timers in a curious, archetypal way—FireMan. Jakey did not come from a guy named Jake, as I had once thought, but from the J-shaped keys that firefighters used to open the corner fire boxes. Smoke-eater—self-explanatory—has a rough, tough edge that I do not relate to.

The little I do know about firefighters is mythical and was learned in childhood. They are knights in brown and yellow armor. They wield axes from roaring red steeds. They charge at fiery dragons, and slay them with wild, piercing cries. As kids, we watched them gallop down the street. *FireMen!* we whispered in awe, letting our ice cream melt down our hands; the name is at once an alleluia and an amen.

Then there is that other myth, the more adult one, laced with admiration and awe, but tinged with a slight disdain, the condescension we reserve for what we do not understand or are excluded from. Because the firehouse is a home and the fire department a family, a culture in and of itself, a private domain, a secret world. This myth says that *FireMen!* are chain-smoking, hard-drinking, *what-the-fuck-do-you-think-you-are-looking-at, boy,* rugged, blue-collared men who save lives.

Not just lives, but babies and homes as well. Babies and Homes! What is more sacred than innocence and property?

You won't fit in. You are not a FireMan!

Suddenly I want to turn around and leave. Was all this a dream? I am a woman, for god's sake. This is a man's world. I cannot picture myself here, in my pressed blue station uniform, treading with the easy relaxed roll of Captain Leahy. I know that I am quick and strong and that fear of shame will keep me brave. But I have no myth of my own to follow, not even a stereotype. I've never pictured a woman as an axe-wielding hero. I've never seen one kick a door in or drive a big truck. I do not smoke, and I've never had a beer.

Could I be a FireMan?

Captain Leahy walks past a small sitting area and then enters a kitchen. He waves his hand for me to enter.

Utensils dangle above a large squat oven. Massive pots and pans line shelves whose doors have been left casually open. In front of me is a long rectangular table, crowded with bread, jars of peanut butter and jelly, some coffee cups, and people. The noise in the room suddenly pivots and stops as faces turn to stare at me.

I have never been the last to be picked for a team, never had my braids pulled in class, never felt the sting of high-pitched laughter as I walk past the "in crowd." I have never been a misfit, a dangling social appendage. But at once I imagine that this is what it feels like not to belong—this enveloping silence, this crush of stares, this heavy discomfort. My mouth feels tight, the rigid smile glued on haphazardly.

The quiet seems to go on forever.

"The Stanford grad," someone finally says.

"The vegetarian," someone else says and laughs slightly.

"Welcome to Station 53." A short, disheveled man comes forward to shake my hand. "Johnny," he offers.

He is older, in his fifties perhaps, with unbrushed black-gray hair. "Come on in, come on in," he insists, and brings his hand up in the air in a large wave motion.

I think that this man must be an angel in clever disguise: his pants are wrinkled, his hair is uncombed and sticks out at the back, and his collar has caught under itself, forming a curve under his ear. His shirt is half-buttoned and askew, as if a great wind has just passed through and tossed him about. A pair of glasses perches unevenly on his nose. He tilts his head to look up at me and then leans back further to bring me into focus.

Johnny suggests that I sit and read the paper, how about some coffee? A man with a double chin and a big belly moves over on the bench, nodding without looking at me directly.

The handshakes and nods begin now in earnest. A round man with hammy hands, fingers blunt like rivets and calloused at the tips, introduces himself as Randy. He has long bushy sideburns, and a bushier moustache. "So your sister is a movie star," he says, not unkindly, and glances around the room as he speaks.

Johnny offers me a tour of the fire station. It is old but comfortable. The furniture is worn, the tiles in the kitchen blur together and the dorm is crowded and dark. Out back there is a small, carefully tended garden.

Johnny is a board member of the Firefighter's Union. I know that the union has fought long and hard against women entering the department and against affirmative action. I remember that it is the union that erased the picture of the black (non-union) member that I had read about while at KPFA. It is also the union that is backing six white male members in their suit against the federal court's consent decree. They have filed an appeal, and have gone so far as to state that the entrance procedure has been simplified for minorities and women to pass. One man claims in the local newspaper that "many of the minorities that they have hired and promoted are not competent."

Despite this, there are valid questions being asked. Can a woman handle the physical demands of firefighting? Is it "fair" and "just" to institute a system of preference based on gender and color, to counter one that once preferred the white male? These are delicate questions, questions that can be construed as sexist and racist. It seems to me that sometimes they are, but sometimes they are not.

From the moment the fire department entered my life, people who know little else about firefighting are sure of one thing: watch out for male firefighters. Watch out for the *firemen*. They are out to harass you.

KPFA staff members tried to talk me out of joining the SFFD, claiming the bigotry would crush me. My mother's first comment was that men from the New York fire department defecated into the boots of female probationers. Even strangers looked at me incredulously when they found out I was in the fire academy, and asked if I had been harassed yet.

How did an institution that stands for courage and self-sacrifice get such a terrible reputation? It would be easy to simplify the situation into the "good guys" and the "bad guys," as each opposing faction has done. And yet, here is Johnny, a member of the "bad" union, showing me, his alleged enemy, around the dorm with casual waves. I make a mental note to keep an eye on my turnout boots.

Johnny points to a bed that I can use each shift with my sleeping bag. Nearby is a portable "privacy screen" behind which I can sleep or change my clothes, since I will have no locker or bathroom of my own. We work 24-hour shifts, and at night I will also be in the same dorm as the men. This doesn't bother me; I had a male roommate in college for a time, but, according to rumor, it bothers some of the wives. I guess I understand, though if one of those wives saw the dormitory, any worries would be laid to rest.

The firehouse dormitory is a schizophrenia of both order and chaos. On the one hand, beds and lockers are lined up in neat rows. But the space is crammed with the remnants of previous shifts: reading lights left on to cast fatigued shadows, ragged paperbacks still open on chairs, old coffee cups, sports pages, overnight bags, unmade beds.

It's perpetually dark, but not in a romantic way. It's as if a dozen dirty blankets have been shaken vigorously, and the dust is still in the air. The only brightness comes from the weak gleam of the brass poles that lead to the apparatus floor below. Ultimately the firehouse dormitory is a functional place designed only for two things: sleep and, once awakened, a fast exit.

Alone in the dorm, I take a deep breath. Pushing aside a *Car and Driver* magazine, I carefully arrange my turnout pants like everyone else's: next to the bed, facing the nearest pole, the legs draped over the boots, and the suspenders untangled and free. Then I sit on the bed I've been given. I wonder if I will sleep tonight, and if I do will I make it into my turnout pants and down the pole to the truck without killing myself? I stand up and look around. When I am sure I'm alone, I step quietly into the boots. Then I hoist the suspenders up and over my shoulders. I pace the steps to the pole—five and a half. I don't slide down the pole, nervous that someone will ask what the hell I'm doing. I step out of the boots and arrange them again.

And so now it begins: I am formally a "probationer," informally a "probie," or even more informally, "probie scum." For the next three months at Station 53, I will be under Captain Leahy's watchful eye, assigned to the fire truck.

Of all the vehicles in a fire department, the fire truck is the most iconic. Snaking through crowded streets, its siren demanding attention, the breadth of it taking up its lane and yours, it bristles with ladders and saws and axes. Miraculously it slides around the tightest corners, thanks to the tiller driver in the back, then thunders down the straight-aways like a charging dragon. Along its back is the fabled one-hundred-foot hydraulic-powered aerial ladder, ratcheted into the bed at rest, but rising on command during the biggest, baddest fires. This ladder is the closest thing to a hand of God a mortal will ever get, as it reaches for high roofs and windows and civilians scramble down its massive length to safety. Sometimes the ladder is more intimidating than the fire, and a civilian will freeze and refuse to go down, and then a firefighter must coax and wheedle and, if necessary, shout. In a really big fire, when the crews are pulled out and the building is in danger of collapsing from the flames, a nozzle is attached to the end for a high vantage of attack, and water rains down from above, soaking everything. Aerials are lowered against windows, breaking them to ventilate the hot smoke and gases, or aimed at a suicidal jumper, then expertly extended, pinning him to the wall with the rungs until he is pulled kicking and screaming to safety.

Suddenly the alarm goes off. I've been waiting for it, but still I'm slammed abruptly with adrenalin, a feeling that will subside only a little over the years. I leap from where I'm sitting on the bed, and dive for the pole.

The alarm, called the Bee-Bop, is not an alarm at all but a loudspeaker that begins with a series of tones. Then a human voice from the dispatch center breaks into the room, indicating the address and type of call. *Street Box 2191*, the voice now says. *Brannan and Third. Street box only.*

I am on the rig before anyone else, bolt upright and breathing hard. My helmet and coat are on, and when the siren starts I feel its sound resonate in my ribs. No wonder Tom is deaf.

I recite the steps I must take if it is a fire: belt, axe, air pack, Chicago door opener. At the corner, I trip out of the seat, my truck belt cinched at the last hole—still too loose—and land on the sidewalk, then look wildly around for the mayhem we have been called to assuage. The axe hangs at my side, its head deep gray and flecked with the spoor of past fires, small nicks and scratches. The axe handle is worn, the grain of the wood smooth and veined. This is the truck person's Excalibur.

"Get on board, rookie," someone says. "False alarm. Just some idiot pulling boxes."

I'm frozen though, expectant, excited.

"False alarm," someone says again. Leahy is motioning to me.

"Oh," I say, embarrassed.

Leahy motions again. "Go on up," he says and points to the til-ler, the legendary steering position of the ladder truck, the one the kids wave to when the long, thin rig goes tearing by like some sort of mad, weaving centipede. Perched on the back end as if on a grand throne, the tiller operator helps the driver by steering the rear of the truck independently from the front, in order to gain wide berth around corners and cars. The current tiller—was his name Doug?—stands up and leans over. He does not say anything as he settles into the training seat. I climb up and the truck slides out onto the street.

I grip the big oval steering wheel. Steering the tiller is a compli-cated affair. It requires you to force the back end away from objects you are being cantilevered toward by the front end, pulling the wheel in the opposite direction of the driver. Beside me Doug looks a little worried. Who can blame him? The back end has no brakes, and the only things at his command are a buzzer he'll push in the event of a mistake by the wide-eyed novice in the seat, and the desperate hope that the driver will hear it and stop in time. Steer opposite, I remind myself, Away From. *Opposite, opposite.*

Off we go.

The only time I relax at all is at red lights. I let the corners of my eyes wander to the sidewalks. People stop, lean down to their kids and point. *Firemen!*

The kids notice first, mid-wave.

It's a girl, they announce to their mothers. *Look, the back one. It's a girl.* The mothers glance up again, poke their husbands' ribs. Whole families stand, catatonic. They don't know what to make of it; their world has shifted a little.

A few days later, Jackie calls. She has had her first fire. "It's so black, blacker than me," she says with exuberance. "The air's so hot, and thick like stew." I try to imagine it, but I can't.

* * *

At my Self-Contained Breathing Apparatus (also known as an SCBA or air pack) drill, I reel off the numbers and parts I've learned. Three thousand psi of air, gauge on bottle, gauge at side. Open it up, lefty-loosey, righty-tighty. Pressure release valve. Arm strap, hip strap. Regulator. Face mask, side straps, top strap.

Captain Leahy nods quietly. He is a good teacher, patient and attentive. Behind me, I hear the sound of laughter, and a high female voice. Randy introduces me to a woman in the neat white uniform shirt of a chief's driver.

Tess is tall, Caucasian, with a big smile and a soft voice. I know that she's from the legendary first class of women, so of course I'm a little in awe. She says hello, then extends one of her hands in welcome.

As I reach to shake it, she pulls it back quickly. She lets out a loud guffaw. My hand is left hanging in the air, my face freezing in shock. I'm momentarily baffled. *What the hell just happened?*

Tess looks at Randy and laughs again. I pull my hand back and let out a quick laugh too. I want to be a good sport, but inside I'm mortified. It was only a small gesture, a second grader's joke, but I feel my face flush, my stomach flip. Tess turns away.

I glance at her as Captain Leahy explains again that when there is a quarter of a tank of air left in the SCBA, an alarm will go off as a warning signal.

"With 90 seconds left of air, the alarm will stop.... "

Did that really happen?

"So when the alarm stops, you'd better be close to a door".

No one told me that I would have to worry about the women too.

To make things worse, today's my day to cook in the firehouse. Everyone is nervous about this. With good reason. I can't cook. I have rarely made a complete meal in my life. I eat only things that are unwrapped, unpeeled or untied. To make matters even more grim, I am a vegetarian.

I have heard legends about these first times, how a probationer will bring in his wife to cook, how the meals can be so bad that they are launched across the room mercilessly, how the worst sin of all is when there is not enough food to go around. The meal is the symbolic center of firehouse culture; to cook a bad meal or worse, a careless one, is blasphemy.

The legends are true: firefighters are excellent cooks, and the Firehouse Meal is an affectionate worship of excess. The tall steaming pots fill plates two or three times. There is loud laughter, funny stories, and perhaps a little urgency, as if the danger of the job is never far from anyone's mind. Passed words, passed food, passed laughter—even to watch as I do, shy and reserved, is an inclusion.

Lunch arrives late in one tall pot. "Vegetarian chili," I say, clearing my throat.

"Where's the beef," someone murmurs as the crew starts to eat politely. But they glance at each spoonful before raising it to their mouths. Afterwards, Captain Leahy says "That was excellent," but he is being kind. Everyone is being kind, and also a little cautious. If I had been male this meal would have been pitched against the wall with theatrical disgust, or thrown up at the ceiling to see if it would stick, but instead there are only jokes about how weak they all feel, how faint from lack of protein.

Just as the dishes are cleared, and the leftover vegetarian chili stored hesitantly in the refrigerator, the Bee-Bop sounds for a "body in the bay."

The body is not in the bay at all, but lying at the end of a cement pier. It is face down and judging by the lividity in the hands, the body is dead. I have never seen a dead body. I stare at the misshapen pile, emotions surging: wonder, curiosity, disbelief. She was once alive, I think stupidly, and now she's not?

A crew is already there and a tall man with glasses shakes his head as we walk up. "Dead. Looks real bad." He glances at me. "You don't want to see it."

In fact, I do want to see it, and take a few steps forward, staring. "She was beaten," the tall man continues, as Captain Leahy leans down and rolls the body over.

The dead woman's eyes are open. Her nose is pushed to one side; her cheeks are mottled green and purple. Her mouth, lined with a garish red lipstick, is swollen and flattened. Her whole face is puffed up to an unimaginable size, so that I am reminded of a Cabbage Patch doll, life-size, discarded. Shocked, I look away to the cheap blonde hair dye with the brown roots showing, and the line where the sun has burned her pale Caucasian skin. She can't be more than 40 years old.

Captain Leahy leans over, presses two fingers against her neck and pauses for the required 5 to 10 seconds. We're silent. She's dead, it's clear, but protocol says you check the pulse anyway, and there's something about the gesture that's important, as if Leahy wants to give the woman the concern in death that she did not have in life. He stands up and coughs. "Let's go home," he says.

As I near the truck, I turn to look one last time. The dead body is still motionless. Did I expect anything else? Death has been just a concept to me; in books, the main character dies heroically; on television the bad guy dies justifiably. Death has meaning—it moves the story, describes the character, precipitates emotion. But here in the real world there is just its banality, cruelty, and anonymity. Later I will see so much more of this, and death will lose any romanticism once and for all. People die in all sorts of compromising positions—during sex, on the toilet, while in the bath—and secrets routinely roll off too—teeth, wigs, hidden fat. Certainly, there are seldom any last words of significance. Even less frequent is the presence of loved ones holding them in a last embrace. Very soon I will see death with a cooler head, hope they had a life well lived, do what I can at the end. But that is then. In my present self, I'm trying to shake off the shock.

"You OK, Paul?" Leahy asks.

I hesitate only a moment. I'm a firefighter now, and this is my new life, and it's just the beginning of all the terrible things I will see.

"Can I tiller, Captain?" I respond, and nod as casually as I can at the back end of the truck.

8.

The glass gives way easily to the axe. It is a satisfying feeling and I stop after the first stroke, listening to the bluster of the window as it leaves the frame before it shatters to the ground. Leahy takes this for hesitation.

"Keep going," he says. "Clear it all out. Always hit the top of the pane, so the glass doesn't come down on your hand." These little tips are obvious, but I never think of them myself. I sweep the frame free, and the night air slides in, smelling of fish and salt.

It is my first structure fire, in an old run-down diner by the water, a place for mariners that looks itself like an old rusty boat, ready to sink. When we arrive there's light smoke showing and Leahy motions for the 35-foot extension ladder. It feels like a feather in my hands, the adrenalin pumping. On the roof, Leahy points to vents and chimneys.

"Knock the tops off," he says.

An old-timer lights up a cigarette. He takes off his gloves and puts his hand on the tar, then exhales thoughtfully. "Ain't hot here," he says.

I want to swing an axe into the roof. "No, no," Captain Leahy says, palm out like a traffic cop. "No sense in making holes if we don't have to." This is a small fire, barely a "room and contents," he tells me. We take the ladder back down.

But now, at overhaul, I have my chance.

Leahy points to the window frame, black and blistered. "Go ahead and remove this. Carefully now. Look at the way it is put together. Take it down that way."

I stare at it. I can swing an axe, but I know nothing about carpentry. Leahy, on the other hand, understands the intentions of the creator. I sense that he, like most firefighters, regards objects that have been built with a spiritual intensity, the process of deconstruction a communion, not a battle. I, on the other hand, just want to demolish it.

"No, no, no," Leahy says as I swing the axe into the middle of the left frame. He sounds offended.

The room quiets. Everyone likes to work, but now they've stopped because here is something more amusing. *The girl's got an axe!*

Some have never seen a woman at a fire before. But there are rumors anyway: how there is no way a woman can swing anything at all, how the head bounces right off the wood, that nothing gets done until a man steps in. But I come from New England, where even the most genteel families chop their own wood. Chopping firewood is part of being a Connecticut WASP; we like the self-sufficiency it implies. My mother, at fifty-four, still chops some of wood she stockpiles, and she's very good with a chainsaw. But these men are not Connecticut WASPS, and many of them have yet to see any of the few female fire-fighters at work.

Leahy steps back. I squint at the frame, trying to look intent, feeling the many stares at my back. I feed the axe into a crack. How on earth do I know how this was put together?

I wonder if I can escape scrutiny if I work silently. I breathe quietly a few times, and pull abruptly at the pick. The wood gives way somewhat with a rubbery feel, not the resounding crack it should have.

"One more time." Leahy doesn't seem to notice that the whole room is watching. "Get the blade in and use the opposite side as a fulcrum."

The room has become so quiet that I imagine I can hear the soft wheeze of wood fibers slowly giving way from water and heat. Okay, the top piece could go next. I bury the impulse to send the axe crashing into it, to overwhelm the audience with light and sound. I cock my head slowly and pretend I am puzzling out the best angle.

Then, without further ado, I bring the axe crashing into it. Before Leahy can say anything else, I swing again, and then again. The frame is in shambles on the floor.

It isn't pretty. It is not even a very good job. I can hear Leahy correct me, point out I am using too much energy, that it can go down with finesse, to try again, slower this time, *look at how it is put together*. I kick the fallen wood out of the way. I nod slowly; we walk to a new window. The men turn back to their work; I hear the hum. *Okay. She can swing. Somewhat. Huh. Yeah.*

On one of my last watches at Station 53, I get my first "greater alarm." It is six in the morning, and our shift is almost done; the dorm lights snap on, and the Bee-Bop begins. *Fire in the building.* I am bolt upright in my bed and then into my boots. Across the room Randy says, "This is it, probie." He knows: a call early in the morning probably means that it is actually a fire, and not a false alarm, and a good fire too, if it caught someone's attention at this hour.

Everyone in the station except me recognizes the address. It is a large brick building, abandoned since the earthquake eight months before. The building's macabre past is vivid in the minds of Station 53 crews: in the earthquake, one of the brick walls gave way and fell on a car that was full of people. Station 53 responded to this call, digging frantically through the wreckage, pulling out the flattened bodies. It is not an address they would forget easily.

Smoke pours out from behind windows blocked by wooden panels. Since the building has been condemned, Leahy calls out that no one is going inside, an order met by curses and bitter complaints. "Come on, boss!" someone yells. San Francisco is fiercely proud of its "interior attack" strategy, and to be prohibited from this building of all buildings is a special affront. Leahy ignores all this and as the ladder we throw against the building quickly catches fire, he waves us even further back. Large lines are set up to "surround and drown" the structure.

As for me, I do what I am told. The fire goes from a single alarm to a second alarm, then a third, and crews arrive from around the city. Sirens wail, horns blare, lights flash, there is shouting, and then the sound of doors slamming and metal hitting metal as nozzles are grabbed, hoses led. All the studying I have done at the academy, all the stories I have listened to about big fires has not prepared me for the real thing—rigs jam the streets, firefighters lope to and fro, a cluster of chiefs crane their heads upward, then consult their clipboards and each other. Hoses snake across the sidewalks, leading who-knows-where, but somehow getting water on the fire. On the surface it's chaos. I'm part of it—grabbing nozzles, hauling line, setting up the aerial. Then the fire goes out, and in go the crews to pull out the debris.

My coat is soaked, my eyes sting, I'm coughing up black phlegm. After it's all over, Leahy puts his hand awkwardly on my shoulder. It is our last time together. He clears his throat and congratulates me on being a hard-working, successful probationer. Then he quickly drops his hand, looks at the ceiling, back at me, and nods.

It is as close to a man-to-man talk as I will get, and I am grateful for it.

9.

To most people, San Francisco is simply a quaint and beautiful city. But to the firefighter, it's a place of imminent danger. The historic wooden houses are easy kindling. The steep hills overwhelm cars, bicyclists, pedestrians. The deep blue Pacific surges onto long beaches, looking for unsuspecting tourists with their heads tilted at the sand or at the sky, to pull out to sea. The majestic cliffs lure walkers, then strand them. Don't get me wrong, firefighters love San Francisco. Most of them were born and raised here. When they give directions they say things like *go down three blocks to where St. Theresa's church was, hang a left at the furniture store that burned in that fifth alarm ten years ago, and past the old warehouse that was near Old Station 4, you know, the one that is now the supermarket.* They know the city like the back of their hand, and with it the particular dangers.

The buildings in San Francisco are made mostly of wood, and sit tightly side by side, like people packed on a bus, shoulders and knees and elbows touching. As a result, when one house catches fire there is always great concern that the surrounding houses, called "exposures", will catch as well. Legendary stories are told of fires gone wild, and whole blocks lost. The only antidote is a swift and cunning interior attack by aggressive firefighters. An interior attack is exactly as it sounds:

firefighters crawl deep into the building looking for the seat of the fire. Other departments think this is crazy, and usually stand outside with hoses, but in San Francisco that "surround and drown" tactic is looked down upon, and used only as a last resort. Interior attacks head off the fire and so they are standard procedure here in San Francisco, even though they are very, very dangerous.

There are other special conditions to watch out for in San Francisco: her streets are steep and narrow. Engines have slipped down hills; a truck once tipped over when its aerial ladder was extended and the side anchors could not be pulled out and secured completely because the street was too narrow. Topography has always interested the San Francisco fire department, who made sure their fire stations were built at the highest elevation possible. In this way the horses that drew the water pumpers could go downhill on the way to a fire; they could slog up the exhausting incline on the way back, when speed mattered less. Horses were often accompanied by Dalmatians, who ran ahead to clear traffic and keep other dogs away. Dalmatians were ideal firehouse dogs, unfazed by the loud bells and noise because of their genial manner and bad hearing. Though the horses and the Dalmatians are long gone, these old firehouses are still in use. They perch like sentinels at the top of steep, narrow streets. Even now it is easy to imagine the large wood doors dragged open and the dogs leaping forward with the horses behind—more than 12 seconds to be harnessed and at the curb was considered too slow—dragging the water pump. Great noise and hullabaloo, not much different from today.

When a fire is reported in San Francisco, a full box goes out over the loudspeakers to the fire stations in that area. The term "full box" refers to the street boxes on many corners of the city, which before the widespread use of telephones was the most common way to summon the fire department. The glass was broken, a hook was pulled, and a series of morse-code-like taps was sent to the dispatch center. The emergency was then reported to stations in a series of bells that mirrored the exact number of the street box, directing responding companies there and therefore to the general vicinity of the emergency. It meant listening to the bells and counting them and then checking a card system to see if your station was due at that box number. If not, the incident still had to be "pegged," or charted on a huge board, so that at any given time each station knew what the others were doing. This was important because your vehicle was responsible for a shifting area of the city, depending on what crews were busy; at any time you might have to fill in if an emergency arose in another district. Now many emergencies are phoned in (though cell pones do not yet exist in great numbers) and modern technology charts the responsibilities of each firehouse. But the city remains divided into box numbers linked to a specific street box. The box number is the first thing that the loudspeaker still says when a fire comes in, but we no longer have to peg boards and we are given the exact address of the incident. As a result, the old-timers are fond of reminding us how tough it used to be and how easy we have it now.

When the fire is reported, a "full box" of furious light and sound descends on the city: three engines, one or two trucks, two chief "buggies," and a Rescue Squad all race through the streets. The rigs arrive in quick succession. The sirens piggyback and for one moment crescendo, then fall silent as feet leave the buttons, helmets and axes are grabbed, doors are flung open, and crews hurtle out. If the fire is big enough ("working fire, give me a second!") another box is struck, and a second alarm goes out. Three more engines, one or two more trucks, another chief. The streets are snarled with fire apparatuses. At a third, the same thing, a fourth, again, and finally a fifth, our biggest fire, where now many blocks in all directions have to be cordoned off from traffic and half the city's firefighters are engaged at keeping it in check. Fire department rigs are often described interchangeably by those who don't know any better, but, make no mistake, the fire engine and the fire truck are two distinct vehicles that do two different but equally important tasks.

The fire engine is the smaller, squattier rig, and its job on a full box is to extinguish the fire. To that end it holds 500 gallons of water, 100 feet or so of 1" hose line, 350 feet of 1'3/4" small hose line, and 1000 feet of 3" large hose line. There are also various brooms, rakes, spanners, and couplings on board. Since the engine is the primary medical unit in the firehouse, unless a Rescue Squad is stationed there, it also carries oxygen, a defibrillator and various other medical equipment.

The fire truck is the long, gangly vehicle, and its responsibility is to ventilate the building of trapped heat and gases, for the safety of the engine crews inside. To that end, it carries wooden ladders on the side and that huge hydraulic aerial ladder along its spine. It blocks the street like a large cannon and shoots its ladder to the roof of buildings for access and evacuation. Inside its compartments are chainsaws and axes and crowbars and a battering ram, so that windows can be broken and holes made in the roofs, and doors pushed open. Traditionally the truck has also been responsible for rescues, though now the SFFD sends a Rescue Squad to every fire, and it's their job to pull people out of buildings.

So here it is again: the trucks use their ladders to access the fire building and perform imminent rescues, and they open the roof with axes or chainsaws to ventilate the heat and smoke. Meanwhile the engine (the crews become their vehicle, so that you are not described as a "member of the engine" but as *the engine*, or *the truck*) is crawling inside with a hose. They battle darkness and heat to find the seat of the fire. *Did ya put water on it*, they are asked when they get home, meaning did they get there first, or did another engine company beat them to it? Putting water on the fire, being way in there and at the very bosom of danger, is the only place to be for an engine.

According to legend, the truck people are big, hairy guys who are loud and reckless. They swing axes, haul chainsaws and throw ladders with gestures as rough as their personalities. Their hands are like the thick slabs of meat and their voice cracks from years of breathing smoke. They're big and loud and exuberant, and this describes my crew at Station 53.

Engine people, on the other hand, are lithe and quick. Legend gives them intelligent, alert eyes constantly half-narrowed as if against smoke, and sinewy bodies to crawl through long hallways. They are easy-going and quieter in the firehouse, and never say a word when their ears singe and their knees get red hot in a fire. Engine people love the hot, greasy breath of danger, and somewhere in their souls is a leaping ferocity.

Firefighters identify themselves with one rig or another and, while I enjoy my time on Truck 53, within a few weeks at Station 91, my new house, I know that I am an engine person.

Smell of smoke, some yelling. Engine 91 is first on the scene with no other engines in sight. My officer is Lt. Doshkov, also known as The Mad Russian. He is not mad so much as high strung, a big change from the pensive, laid back Captain Leahy. Doshkov is the quintessential engine person: small and lean and aggressive. He is known to suddenly lose his temper, but not in an emergency situation. As we pull up to the address and see smoke trickling out the left door, Doshkov is out of his seat and onto the street before the engine has even stopped.

Patricia is quicker than I am and has the nozzle in her hand while I am still putting on the SCBA. I met her this morning, my first day at Engine 91. She stood in front of me and sized me up with narrowed eyes. At almost six feet tall and solidly built, Patricia is intimidating.

I clear my throat to explain myself, but Patricia's expression makes it clear that she's not at all interested in anything I have to say, now or ever.

"As long as you're not a wimp," she says, by way of introduction. There's no small talk, no how-are-you, where-are-you-from niceties. But I don't care. Patricia has been in the firehouse for a few years now.

She belongs to the first class of women, and thus is one of the First Women In. As one of The First Women In, she has quasi-immortal status in my eyes, and quasi-immortals hold secrets I need to know. Tess, who had also been in that class, had been rude too, but she had also never bothered to speak to me. Patricia has advice, and I want to hear it.

"And don't, for god's sake, flirt. That looks bad for all of us." Patricia worked for years on an ambulance, picking up pieces of people in some of the toughest neighborhoods in the country. She was a cement layer before that. She is now a firefighter, something she has wanted since she was five years old. She's married to a sheriff, and together they ride big motorcycles through winding mountain roads. All this to say that Patricia is tough, and blue-collar life runs in her veins.

Patricia is supposed to give me the hose since I'm the probationer and this is how we learn to fight a fire, but she doesn't. She charges in, and I follow. The apartment is narrow and smoky, but Patricia seems to know where to go, even though visibility drops to almost nothing halfway down the hall. I am right behind her when she stops suddenly and yells, "More line!" I stand there, not understanding, and she yells, "More line!" again. I turn and run out, past the engine driver who stands on his heels with his arms crossed, a crooked cap on his head. "We need another line," I say, and he looks surprised. I am back into the building before anything more can be said, the nozzle in my hand.

Afterwards, Patricia explains that "More line" means to pull the existing hose around the corners, up the stairs, anything so that the nozzle person can advance easily. It does not mean to get another line, as I did.

"You sure are dumb, for a goddamn Stanford graduate," she says. I hang my head. "But you were pretty fast," she adds, and I think I hear approval in her voice.

It is this way with fighting fire: you learn on the job, and a real fire is much more than a triangle diagram.

I am lucky that Patricia decides to take me under her wing. She gives me the tips that she wished she had gotten two and a half years ago, when she first came in. These are not tips that come with drills, but unspoken codes that are played out at each fire. The first rule, Patricia says, is Never Give Up your Equipment.

"Then where are you? Empty handed and frigging useless. A goddamn maiden in distress." She gives me a withering look. "If someone asks for your axe or your ceiling hook, tell them, fuck off, fella, I'll do it. Have them point out what they need the equipment for and, Jesus Christ, do it yourself."

"But, uh, that doesn't sound like *teamwork*. What if, well, someone else is in a better position to swing the axe than I am?" I ask this quietly, unwilling to lose my tentative foothold on her esteem. Patricia scowls and shrugs. These are the rules. And there is a meaning behind them. To give up your equipment means that you don't want to do the work, and doing the work—being the first into the fire and the last out—is an old tradition. In 1850, two volunteer firefighters from different companies crawled into a burning hospital to check that no one was left inside. They became trapped from behind by flames. The two men, both officers, managed to chop a hole in the roof and climb to safety. "You first," said the officer from the St. Francis Hook and Ladder. "No, I insist," replied the officer from Protection Engine #6, "You first." They stood their ground and each refused to exit before the other, knowing that the final honor is to leave last, even as the flames quickly caught up to them. I do not know how this was resolved. My guess is that they squeezed through the hole together.

Fine, I won't give up my equipment.

"Never say you are scared, either," Patricia continued. "If you want to process, process somewhere else."

I like this advice. Fear can be corrosive, and to dwell on fear is more corrosive still.

"And if you don't know what to do, do something. Go forward. Don't just stand there like a deer in headlights."

Done with her advice, Patricia walks away.

Unlike Station 53, Station 91 is a single engine company with a chief and a chief's aide. There are six people instead of eleven, and it's a busy station. I am happy to be here, ready for more work.

Just as I learned to drive, operate and take care of the fire truck at Station 53, now I have to learn to drive, operate and take care of the fire engine. That responsibility falls on Thomas, the engine driver on my shift.

Thomas has been a San Francisco firefighter for over twenty years, and his father was a San Francisco firefighter before him. By his own admission he was vehemently against women coming into the department. But like any man who believes in machinery, he knows that the true test is if it works when put together. If he sees that it does, he's willing to change his mind.

Working with Patricia changed his mind.

So now he's earnest about teaching me how to be an engine driver. It's a difficult job, and it's the heart of the firefighting operation, or to take the analogy even further, the sino-atrial node, in charge of signals for the ornery heart, called the pump. The pump resides in the engine and to get to it means pulling, pushing, and twisting at dials on the side of the rig.

The primary blood for this heart is, of course, water. While there is 500 gallons of water to draw from in the tank on the engine, it will only last as little as a minute and a half if a big line is used, three and a half minutes if small lines are used. The primary water source is the hydrant. Attaching a hose (or the vein, following the analogy) from the hydrant into the engine, the engine driver then adjusts for pressure and volume, sending the water out through different hoses. While this might sound fairly straightforward, it must be done while a building is burning up in front of you. Little things, like locating the hydrant and making the small dial adjustments for water pressure, become major feats amidst flames and heat and the cries of panicked residents. Water pressure in the hose is supposed to be between 80 and 100 pounds per square inch (psi), but excited drivers have been known to accidentally dial 200 pounds or more. This much pressure will immediately throw down whoever is on the nozzle, which now bucks like a wild bronco. If you're holding that nozzle while on a ladder, or a roof, well, it isn't going to be pretty.

Water goes in, water goes out. While I know this is true, it doesn't demystify the process for me. Perhaps it's because to be an engine driver is to be a particular kind of firefighter. It's a job of steady and precise dance moves—step to the hydrant, swing left with the spanner, swing right with the hose coupling. What's more, the engine driver is the proverbial person behind the scenes, integral but robbed of glory: the gaffer not the director, the roadie not the rock star, the wife not the great man in front of her.

Many firefighters become engine drivers because they love the mechanics of pumping water, but some become engine drivers after they have been badly burned in fires; to my knowledge, this has never happened to Thomas, but he has been shot. During the race problems in the '70s, the National Guard accompanied the fire crews, their guns drawn. Thomas was hit by a bullet on the way to a call. The scar on his left arm is visible as he reaches for the outlet gate #3, patiently going through the procedure with me one more time.

The woman has a pulse, but it's weak and thready. Her color is pale, and she's breathing shallowly.

"What's her name?" I ask the staff, who have gathered around, wide-eyed. I'm the probie, so I have to run the medical calls. Already I'm flustered, because the woman's eyes are open, but she's not responding. Then the only oxygen bottle the nursing home had was unaccountably empty, so when we arrive nothing has been done. Now I'm asking her name and this is met with uncomfortable shuffling, a shifting of eyes, shrugs all around.

"We don't know her name," one of the staff says, averting his gaze.

We are at the Sunnyside Hacienda, which is not sunny at all. It is horizon-flat, stuck casually between two old Victorian houses. I have never been inside a home for the elderly, but I expected it to look like the one in the movie *Cocoon*, full of spry old folk lining the hallways and chatting amiably among each other.

There are no spry people in the hallways, and no one sits up in bed to greet us. None of these people can sit up, few can even talk. Hospital beds are lined up in rows, four to a room. IV stands glint in the light from the hallway, like stern nurses beside their charges, whom I cannot see, as if they have become part of the bed itself. The staff wear white coats, but we all know they're not doctors, just minimum-wage workers dressed to look so for family members who may visit once in a while. The doctor on call, they tell me, does not answer his page.

"Then can I see this woman's medical history?" I say. Next to me, Mike shifts his feet. He has a pugilist's face and big, square hands to go along with it. He doesn't speak to me beyond a polite hello in the mornings. I can't tell if this is just the way he is, or if he does not like a woman in the house, so I decide to assume the former.

Someone steps forward and admits they can't find the woman's medical chart.

"This place is the pits," Mike says under his breath.

The paramedics arrive, breathing heavily from the weight of their bags, which they drop with a loud thud. One paramedic, thin and pale with a thatch of black hair, leans over the bed.

"Huuu-nnney," he croons to the woman. "Can you hear me?" He flaps his hand in front of her face. No response. An airway tube is inserted unceremoniously down her throat. With a practiced flourish it's taped into place, so that the woman's cheeks bulge and her lips splay out at awkward angles. She is trussed for rescue. Working fast, one medic slaps at her arm to get a vein to rise, the other drops a stethoscope onto her chest.

Mike hands me the oxygen bag valve mask and I start pressing it, my job now to push oxygen into her. Her eyes are open. They stare at me, seeing me, I am sure of it.

I want to say: *are you scared? if you are, that's okay too.* Or *are you comfortable? Should I move the sheets?* Hearing is the last to go, we're told, so what's the harm? But I don't say any of that, of course I don't. I don't want to sound foolish, or girlish, or odd. I glance at her hand on the arm that isn't being scrutinized for needle placement. The skin seems translucent, and I can see her intimate inner workings—the blue veins, the thin strands of bone, the pads of muscle. I imagine that at this moment she is trapped inside an immovable body, frightened of the tumult around her, unable to speak. If I hold her hand, or say something to those eyes, I can make it better. I imagine the seventy years of her life, and think how she deserves this, at least.

"Okay, Okay," is all that I finally murmur. I lean in and say it as the paramedic pricks her arm for a vein and keeps an eye on the heart monitor. Just take her hand, my mind admonishes, while another part of me is acutely aware of Mike nearby and what he might think. The fact that she might have heard that this nursing home attendant does not know her name offends me deeply, but I am too concerned about my professional image as a firefighter to do the things I want to do to help her through what seems inevitable at this point: death. I wonder what Patricia would do. I stare at the woman's hand and squeeze the oxygen bag instead.

When the cart starts to move I tell myself that this is my chance, that no one will notice. The hand, which seems so frail that the slightest movement might float it off the bed, stays put on her hip. I stare at it, but I don't make my move. I will say something instead. I will tell her where we are going, that she will be fine. That it is raining lightly, but tomorrow it is supposed to be sunny. That the staff does know her name, but it doesn't mean anything, not really, they're just flustered and unused to all this commotion.

I never hold her hand. I don't say much of anything. I just pump oxygen into her and she dies on the way to the hospital. I know when she dies, as if her soul brushed by my eyelids and patted my hair. I lean back on my heels and listen to the siren.

Later, when I am alone, I cry. It is a slow quiet weep, a molting, more of illusion. How could I have given in so easily to insecurity, to fear of emotion, to fear of death? Suddenly it's clear: my ability to fly planes, or raft the biggest whitewater, or crash down ice walled chutes means very little. Clearly, I remain less than average where courage may matter the most.

In a fire, the crews work together in unison. There is a formula that we learn: where the first engine goes (in front and a little forward of the fire building), where the second engine goes (to a hydrant to supply water to the first engine), where the first truck goes (in front of the fire building, behind the first engine). We learn what the engine crew does (enter the fire building with a hose) and what the first truck crew does (help with rescue, ladder the fire escape, ventilate). But it is the individual acts of heroism and courage that really put out the fire, the small movements within the mandates. Tonight, I remembered all the medical protocol, but I forgot the most important thing—that once, another firefighter found the courage to hold a woman's hand while a building burned.

10.

When the alarm comes in for Masonic and Grove, it is late afternoon. There is nothing faster than the speed with which firefighters dash to the rig when a full box comes in. Fire! we think. Fire! we hope. The pole holes open with a crash like thunder and bodies drop through as if from heaven. Doors swing wide and other bodies plunge past; they grab coats, fire helmets, flashlights as they go.

We attend to our other duties—medical calls, lockouts, water leaks, car accidents—with integrity. But fire is the call we're waiting for. This is not to say that we love the destruction that a fire wreaks, but that when a fire happens, we want to be there.

At my 1989 department graduation, the mayor of San Francisco gave a speech. At the time, he was determined to dismantle the "old" fire department; it was under his leadership that public pressure and constant media coverage plagued the institution. He heartily disliked the department, and his presence as a keynote speaker was a special affront. Number 28 sat next to me with his fists pressed together and his head bowed, offended that this man who accused the department of racism and sexism was speaking on this special day.

The Caucasian mayor recalled a fire that had happened years before in which a child had died. The fire was in a black neighborhood which, full of grief and loss, accused the white fire department of taking their time getting to the fire. This misunderstanding, he said, was only one example of why an integrated department was so important.

The mayor said that he himself was sure that firefighters had arrived at that tragic fire as fast as they could. Nevertheless, his speech opened a wound. Few incidents are as painful to a firefighter as the death of a child at a fire, but the accusation that not enough was done may be one of them. A firefighter plunges willingly into a dangerous situation, risking his or her life for a stranger and a stranger's property. The mayor's point that day had validity, but it was lost in what many firefighters really heard. They heard the accusation that they had not responded quickly or bravely enough because the neighborhood was black and they were white.

But it takes only a few days in a firehouse to realize that this is virtually impossible. When the call for a fire comes in, there is no hesitation. There is a rush for the rigs, a mad scramble to get out the door. No matter how prejudiced a firefighter might be, it simply doesn't come into play here. The only thing on everyone's mind is fighting fire.

Station 91 is half a minute away from Grove and Masonic. When we pull up, thick black smoke is already spewing from an open doorway. A man is doubled over and gasping. Later, I will learn that this is an off-duty San Francisco firefighter who tried to rush in but was kept back by the intense heat and smoke. Near the doorway people are screaming and pointing, and one woman is being restrained from running back in. Someone else crouches on the sidewalk and wails.

Lt. Doshkov is not working today. In his place is Lt. Murphy, nice enough but nervous, speaking with a slight stammer, with movements of his head and hands that are jerky and charged. The only thing loose about Lt. Murphy is his skin, which hangs morosely from his cheeks and around his eyes. Now he's hesitating at the air packs, so I don't wait. Patricia is already at the hose bed.

The probationer is supposed to be given the nozzle for experience and this time Patricia hands it to me and begins to pull line. I tuck it under my arm, run up the stairs and at the top, as the smoke suddenly thickens, I kneel to put on my air mask. Lt. Doshkov appears, a ghostly outline, and kneels too. Only a couple feet ahead, visibility narrows to a filament and then disappears. I can already feel the heat.

Blacker than me, and thick like stew, I hear in my head. I can't see anything, but I crawl forward anyway. I am first in, where every engine person wants to be, first in, with the nozzle. In front of me there's smoke and, somewhere, the seat of the fire.

My officer is saying something to me. I hear only a muffled yelling from behind his air mask. "What? What?" I shout, but it comes out an elongated, flattened sound that falls away into the dark. He presses his mask close to me, striking my helmet. This time I hear him a little better, and then he is gone, back down the stairs.

All this has taken seconds. Gone? Where could he go? Is this a test? Later I will find out that he forgot his flashlight and went back down to the fire engine to get it. Why he needs a flashlight in this impenetrable smoke is beyond me. Nevertheless, there is now only one thing to do. To do anything else would mean that I am afraid: I keep going.

Immediately, I am swallowed up in the smoke. I can't see my gloves, my coat, even the rim of my air mask on my face. I'm struck suddenly with the absurd thought that I have disappeared. Somewhere Patricia is pulling line behind me, but I feel utterly alone. And it is hot. I know the numbers: 300 degrees one foot above the floor, 500 degrees five feet above the floor, 1200 degrees at the ceiling. I drop lower.

This is a black that is so black it starts to assume shapes, as if the brain cannot stand the nothingness any longer. Which is why a few seconds later, I begin to think that I can see.

In the coming years I will have a different approach. If I hit something as I crawl I will concentrate on getting around it, and ignore the mind games that darkness plays. I will refuse to name whatever I've just bashed into; maybe it's a table or a chair or a bed, but I don't care—in the moment it will be something that just needs to be circumvented. If I do try to name it, then it'll immediately take on a faux reality. I'll struggle to cast aside a chair, and then realize it's actually a huge bed. Instead the mind has to remain supple, preconceived notions pliable.

But right now I'm just a rank novice, and a rank novice alone, in the dark, to boot. So when I run into something and rear back, surprised, it's no wonder I immediately try to figure out what the offending object is. I half stand, and it hits my legs, and so I decide this must be a stairway, and I crawl onto it. Standing now, ignoring the heat, I try to step up, but I hit something ahead of me. Sure that this must be a small attic space, I step up and lunge forward as if to squeeze into a hole. Again I hit something and my feet find no step. Insistent, I lunge again, and perhaps again, rapping my head hard each time. All this happens quickly, and then I feel a hand on my coat, pulling. Someone is behind me. The hand, all-knowing and seemingly all-seeing (or, more likely, adjusted to non-seeing) guides me to the left and we crawl down what must (it must!) be a hallway. The heat heightens. Shafts of lightning streak out in front of us.

Flames in an un-vented fire don't look like what you would expect. There is no booming orange flare, only slivers of non-black that dart and disappear like hallucinations. I spray the nozzle above us, in wide circles and then at the streaks of light. We advance at a half crouch, sometimes bumping into things. *Breathe slowly,* I try to remind myself. *Slowslowslow.* I don't want the alarm on my air pack to go off too soon, signaling low air. *Scared,* the other crews would say, *Sucked all her air. Goddamn hyperventilated.*

The heat is worse now, and we lie flat, bellies on the floor, air bottles like shells on our backs, hot water hitting the ears, the neck, soaking our pants, our gloves. The thick protective leather on our

hands inhibits touch. The black smoke muffles sound and sight. We can smell only the rubber lining of our air masks, but not much else. Every sense is dulled. Yet something leaps in me when The Hand and I turn and there, in a wide grin of light, is the fire full force. This is the room where it started, now "fully involved."

There are more people behind me, yelling and pushing. Everyone wants to see the fire; everyone wants to face it head on. At my side, I hear my alarm go off. I pass the nozzle reluctantly to The Hand and follow the hose out.

The smoke clears quickly once windows are broken and the roof chopped open. By the time I return with a new bottle on my back, the apartment has taken form. The staircase where I knelt to put my mask on is covered with a thin green rug. A wooden banister climbs up one side. I walk around the bend and up to the landing.

One glance tells me that it is no attic stairway that I was on. Instead, in a far corner, a single chair is propped against the wall. A sharp breath escapes me. *Jesus, no. I was there, on the chair.* I was not getting into an attic. I was butting the wall. Momentarily, I was a disoriented cow. I was Quixote, mistaking a windmill for a knight; I was from the middle ages, sure that the line of the horizon was the edge of the flat world.

Thank goodness for the pitch black. No one else, not even The Hand, could see me.

The Hand turns out to be the chief's aide, or "operator," a tall lanky man with a long, lanky mustache to match. His job is to be the eyes and ears of the chief, who stands outside and directs the fire crews. Inside, the operator relays fire information: the seat of the fire, its extent, its special hazards. It can be an undemanding job, according to the most grizzled of firefighters. Often the operator stands outside with a clipboard, in effect a secretary for the chief. But the first chief on the scene sends the operator in, and then the operator's job is something else altogether. Without a hose or an axe, only a radio, the operator must be both savvy and brave. Today, the operator has plucked me from darkness (and humiliation) and led me with a seeming sixth sense to the fire.

As if I have summoned him with my thoughts, he suddenly materializes near me and I look away from the chair. Does he know? If he does, I see no sarcasm in his eyes; he simply asks me where the hell my officer went. I shrug.

"You shouldn't have gone in there alone," he says.

The body is hard to find at first, until someone steps on her among the debris and ashes and her intestines surge up like an orchid trying to bud. Someone tells me to come see, and I do. She doesn't look like anything human, just an effort of color—white, red—against the black ash. The smell is distinctive, like sour barbecue. Later, I will find that the smell clings to my coat, and I wonder if flecks of skin are lodged there in the seams, if I crawled over her in the blackness.

Afterward, they will find the fire extinguisher melted beside her, which means that she died conscious and fighting. The fire started from her cigarette smoke: ash that she flicked into the wastepaper basket smoldered, silently igniting the curtains. From there the fire spread quickly, efficiently. Asleep perhaps, the woman only noticed when the chair caught fire. Or when her hair was burning. At some point she grabbed the fire extinguisher. By then, it was far too late.

Outside, a woman is being restrained as she is told the news. She screams at the chief and then swears at him, her agony rising and falling until she runs out of breath. She is black and he is white, a scenario relived. "You came too slow," she says over and over.

During overhaul Patricia goes into a repeated tirade about *how in the fucking world* a probationer could have been left by an experienced officer. *How in the fucking world*, she says again, swinging her axe. I know she is more relieved than angry, relieved that at least I did not follow him down like a scared puppy. Instead, I went into the fire all alone. *Stupid thing to do*, she murmurs to me, but I can tell she is glad.

No one says anything to Lt. Murphy. It is the code; some things are better left unacknowledged. As for me, I don't care. I'm exhilarated that I had the nozzle.

The fire *belongs* to the person at the nozzle, who is First In. Those who are First In are the ones who face the real danger. The real danger is uncertainty. Those behind have the security of knowing that the person ahead is still alive, and they have that extra chance that the person ahead won't get if something goes wrong.

Despite this, no one I know wants to be behind. To be First In is to be the bravest.

Finally Patricia stops railing. She leans on her axe and appraises me. "Good job," she says, "for an idiot."

11.

I pick up my fire helmet. Its true, the paint is streaked in wide brush strokes and Billy says that it looks terrible, that he'll paint it for me himself. I agree, it does look pretty bad. But I did it on my own, and that is enough. We prize our helmets, and paint them carefully, if not skillfully: red and white if you are on the truck, black if you are on the engine, black and white if you are on the Rescue Squad.

Once painted, small tokens are affixed: green Irish clovers, American flag stickers, playing cards. For me, a small gold angel, made of plastic and a gift from my godson, is pinned near a particularly crusty paint streak. In a good hot fire, this angel will probably melt into an almost imperceptible dribble, but I want it anyway. They're superstitions, these good luck charms, but comforting anyway. Most firefighters believe in God, but also Lady Luck, and a little bit of mere chance. Perhaps some magic. Why not? When all hell breaks loose, it's best to have the bets hedged, our options open.

Helmets are pragmatic too, of course. Things are always heading toward you from above: embers, tools, glass, wood. I had a roof fall in on me, and once an explosion sent the crew just ahead of mine reeling back into us. But the helmets are beautifully made for these eventualities. The bucket is hard, to protect the head, the curved rim keeps hot water off the neck, and the shield in front and colors on the sides indicates the rig and crew to which you belong.

Once, last year, when I was still on probation, I forgot to put my helmet on. My officer noticed it just as I was advancing the line down the hallway ahead of him, and the film of smoke was turning thick black. He ordered me out of the building immediately, but in the commotion I pretended not to hear. I didn't want to leave, for one, and for two, I knew how it would look if I exited the building before anyone else. I much preferred a charge of insubordination to an accusation of cowardice, and in the end I just received a stern talking-to.

Helmets can't protect from animosity, though. I hear early on that there is at least one station that has made a formal pact not to speak to women. Ironically, stories are told in the firehouse about men who, in the days when cocktail hours were openly condoned in the firehouse and many of the men drank, would pass out and have to be put to bed. There was no secret pact against them. There are men so out of shape that after they throw a ladder they must lean against it, breathing heavily. There's no secret pact against them. So it is strange to me that the women have been singled out by this station, even though some of them have never even met us.

I know that the exclusion is not always deliberate. Men have a "ritualized" interaction that differs strongly from the "ritualized" interaction of most women. According to some studies, the male culture is strictly hierarchical, so boys learn quickly that it is important to maintain one's position by self-promotion and the putting down of others, often in jest. This continues into manhood, and becomes obvious in the firehouse, where many conversations involve hair loss, belly girth, or sly comments about the other man's wife. Sociologists call this a "ritual of opposition"; the firehouse calls it "slamming".

Conversational rituals for women, on the other hand, are not hierarchical. Instead, we concentrate on maintaining an appearance of parity. We take the temperature of the room constantly, and make certain that everyone in the vicinity feels fine and equal, even if this means putting ourselves down in order to achieve it. This begins early: girls are not often rewarded for standing out. As we grow up it remains important to be diffident and gracious. So women say they're sorry when they didn't do anything wrong, thank you when they've received nothing, and I'm Really Happy to Hear That even when it's clearly not true. It's no wonder communication between the genders is so confusing.

One day Billy tells me about a "slam" that highlights the differences in our ritualized socialization. Billy says that he suspected that his wife was having an affair with a Spanish language teacher. Extremely agitated, he asked his officer for permission to sneak home and check if his suspicions were justified. Sure enough, he walked in on his wife in bed with her lover. Billy returned to the firehouse in shock. He stumbled around in a daze, and soon the whole firehouse knew that Billy had caught his wife with the Mexican professor. That night when dinner was served, everyone got steak and potatoes. Except Billy. The chef made him a plate of burritos, rice and refried beans.

"Are you serious?" I exclaimed, when he finished telling me the story. He had a smile on his face, but I was beginning to sputter. "That is so, so, *cruel*." Not to mention racist.

Billy looked at me in surprise. "Naah. They were just trying to make me feel better," he said. "It was funny, they made me laugh."

"I see," I said, not seeing at all.

Neither the male nor the female way of interacting is wrong, or bad. As sociologist Deborah Tannen points out in her study on gender interaction in the workplace: "When everyone is familiar with the conventions, things work well. But when ways of speaking are not recognized as conventions, they are taken literally, with negative results." Imagine how hard it is, for both men and women, when conversational rituals that they have taken for granted encounter a different rite.

To make matters worse, it is hard for either gender to join in the other's rituals. If a woman tries to slam, she is regarded as "unlady-like" by both men and women. Similarly, if a man is intent on mak-ing another man feel his equal, thus downplaying his own attributes, he risks being regarded as a wimp. So the uncertainties that a minor-ity member can feel in an otherwise homogenous group is not only the result of malice, intentional exclusion, or outright resentment. It's because important ritualized behavior is not shared. This cycle feeds on itself, and as women and men, blacks and whites, fail to communi-cate with each other, each blames the other for not trying hard enough to understand and connect. This is difficult to change. Interacting with people like oneself, who understand and use the same conversation ritual, is more fun. It is easier. I know: I begin to realize that this is what I have done all my life. Until now my friends have been overwhelm-ingly white, college educated, upper middle class, and WASPy—basi-cally social twins. This makes my past almost as culpable as the fire department's past.

But let's face the truth: there still are people who purposely want to inflict hurt. And it's not hard to do. While the law tries to deal with silent exclusion—"shunning" is the technical term and it is prohib-ited—it is easy to interact in small, clipped sentences as if every word is an effort or, more commonly, to talk nonstop to the people nearby as if the outsider were invisible. The point is made loud and clear.

Meanwhile, those who do not fear the brunt of this exclusion have the luxury to laugh about shunning. "I'm in trouble if I say something, I'm in trouble if I don't," they groan. "Now does that make sense?" People complain that their conversations are inhibited, that they must always "watch out." The firehouse, once a haven for the rituals of all-white male conversation, must now include women and people of color.

Do these white men have a good reason to hate us? Of course not. Do I understand their bitterness? Yes.

It is important to understand their position. These are able people, with families for whom they want to make a good life. Suddenly, promotional exams for which they have studied hard are declared "culturally biased." In 1984, for example, when not enough minorities passed an exam for the position of lieutenant, it was suspended to ensure that the test be deemed fair. To those white males who had put in many hours a day preparing for this test, the statistical analysis that showed "disparities sufficient to establish a prima facie case of discriminatory hiring and promotion under Title VII" was empty semantics. It sounded like the long-winded whining of people who couldn't score well. Even though the city admitted that the "tests used were not demonstrably job-related," the white male firefighter had studied hard and done well. Suddenly an outside institution, which didn't know how to chop a hole in the roof or run a pump panel, was telling him what makes a "job-related" test.

On the other hand, there are insidious facts that cannot be overlooked. By 1974, there were only four black firefighters among 1800 whites. Women were not allowed to take the test until 1976, and none were hired until 1987. Since 1970, the courts have asked San Francisco's civil service unit on three separate occasions to justify their tests, which were repeatedly found not to be job-related. The city did little to change them; the courts declared themselves finally "fed up." In 1987, the U.S. District court ruled that "this sorry history will come to an end." Lawyers armed with the Consent Decree were to manage the fire department; certain "goals" of women and minorities would now be met in hiring and promotion.

How else could it have been done? The fire department was given at least three opportunities to change on its own. The department dragged its feet in the recruitment of women and people of color. The result is affirmative action.

As a woman, my experience in the SFFD is mine alone. Other women and people of color, here and in other departments, have experienced things that I have not. Some have had a really tough time; others say that they have never had an uncomfortable moment in a firehouse—all these experiences are valid. Mine happen to be somewhere in between.

I have been told by one officer that I cannot drive the truck until he sees me swing an axe. What does swinging an axe have to do with driving a fire truck? Meanwhile, he lets a man junior to me drive—whom he also has never seen swing an axe. In just two months, this driver gets into two accidents. Nevertheless, the officer keeps the junior man at the wheel, waving off my requests. I do not profess to be a good driver—in fact I am a lousy one, but no worse, surely, than my hapless peer. Only when I take the officer aside does he finally start to back-peddle.

He sputters and mutters and finally, understanding that his position is untenable, abandons his lame excuses. I drive the next watch, though now my new burden is to "prove" that I am worthy.

Another time I am told that I am "turning on the guys" when I wear the normal uniform t-shirt. In yet another instance, mild come-ons are whispered to me by a firefighter as he passes by.

But most of my encounters have been more subtle exclusions and discomforts, a kind of insidious interaction difficult to explain to anyone who has not experienced it. People want breasts tugged, lewd words spoken, drooling hyena laughs. But there are far less obvious manifestations of prejudice, and I know them when I see them.

Once, I stop by another station with a notice that needs to be posted on their bulletin board. The man who opens the door stands with his arms folded across a gigantic belly. His eyes are deliberately expressionless. There is not a trace of friendliness, not even of recognition, though he knows that I am a fellow firefighter. He blocks the door, legs spread wide, one shoulder against the door jam, hands in fists. The scene strikes me as ludicrous.

"I'll do it," he says reaching for the piece of paper in my hand. His voice has an edge; he doesn't like even having to talk to me. In case

I don't understand, he sneers, then shifts to block the door further, so that I get the message loud and clear.

Get out. You're not welcome here.

Prejudice at its best is like this. It does not raise its voice or shout. It makes you doubt your own sense of reality. Afterwards, if you try to explain it, the thrust and weight of its insult cannot be accurately conveyed. That is the point: prejudice bypasses the verbal synapses, and makes its sly, slow, insidious crawl straight into the trenches of your confidence.

As a twin, I understand the use of body language. An identical twin knows instinctively that the way a word is said and the smallest of posture changes differentiates you from your same-looking sibling. We are attuned to these because they define us, make us separate. We know their power, and when they are used by others, we recognize them. With identical twins, it is hard to actually pinpoint what the difference is, only that there is one; likewise, a person's prejudgment is obvious, but hard to describe. People who do not experience prejudice sometimes doubt those who do; they see them as over-reactors, manipulative and humorless.

But step into a room full of people where you are hopelessly different and you will understand immediately.

A few years ago, the red fire engine was briefly painted a different color in some cities. It was an odd hue, a glaring yellow-green that gave the impression of neon. Studies had determined that this particular color was easier to distinguish than any other color; it would be safer for civilian traffic and for the speeding fire crew.

It soon became apparent that although this yellow was easier to see, a citizenry accustomed to red fire engines did not react as expected. The new yellow color meant nothing to them or to their reflexes. The old red fire engine held a unique place in their minds, one that defied studies and facts.

It's in this way that some firefighters hold fast to their prejudgments of color or gender no matter how much individual job performance proves them wrong. To be a black or an Asian or a woman means that you have gotten your job unfairly, that you are unqualified.

But this is not a matter of easy rights and wrongs, so best to pause from holding only the fire department up to the light. After all, the fire department is both a product of the culture that employs it and a mirror of the country's problems.

That the San Francisco Fire Department had hired only five blacks by 1975 is more a telling commentary on racism in America. Even the achievements of the Civil Rights Act in 1964 could not erase inequities with the stroke of a pen. The fact that women were not allowed to apply to the fire department until 1976 is not surprising either: only one in twenty five girls were encouraged to play high school sports at that time. If physical activity was not considered something a girl could do in our society, why would the fire department want to hire women to perform such intensely physical work?

This does not excuse the problems. But firefighters have always made us question ourselves. We watch them run into a burning building and we wonder, "Could I do that? Am I that brave?" Forget the finger pointing—*that racist, sexist fire department!* There is a lot to learn from San Francisco's Jakeys, and the first step is to admire, as I do, the way they have struggled to handle change and diversity. Face it: we all surround ourselves with people who look, talk and act as much like us as possible.

Really, few of us have had to encounter such an abrupt and uncomfortable shift in our daily life.

I ask, *Could I do that? Am I that brave?*

12.

With two years in, I am no longer a probationer. I start to feel more comfortable when I go to work; the sharp smell of gasoline and ash is familiar and the undercarriage of the engine, with its joints and springs, makes some sense. Firehouse life becomes easier.

On the first day at my new station, an old-timer pushes his hand out on the table in front of me. The skin is gnarled and twisted like the grain of an old tree. The old-timer, whose name is Bunker, stares at me. "This is how far I go in," he suddenly says. "Are you with me?" I stare at his burned hand.

"Of course," I say.

We have just come back from a call where a woman dialed 911 to complain of alien disturbance. When we arrived she pushed aside a heavily curtained window. She pointed to a nearby chimney. "Laser beams are coming from there," she said. "They don't think I know, but I do."

She claimed that it was causing a sticky goo-like substance to seep through the walls, so I ran my hand along the paint. I nodded at her, though I could see or feel nothing out of the ordinary. We helped her fortify the tin foil she had stuffed in the window cracks.

Bunker continues to stare at me, his burned hand forward as if to make sure that I understand its import. I stare back, unmoving. "Okay," he finally says.

Soon after, I take Bunker's detail. A "detail" is when a crew member from a station that is overstaffed is sent to one that is understaffed. "Details" balance the workforce each day. Today I'm sent to Station 60, which houses just an engine. I arrive as details do, hat in hand, tie in place, overnight bag on my shoulder. The captain who is about to go off duty greets me with a big smile. This is in itself not unusual, as Captain Viviani is a jovial man. What is odd is that he has a camera in his hand and seems all ready to use it.

When Wendy and Susan walk in holding coffee, I finally understand. Susan is the driver, Wendy is the firefighter, and I am the other firefighter, which means … it's the first all women SFFD crew. Only our officer is a man—poor guy, I think. He'll be hammered all day today.

We agree good naturedly to take pictures. Why not? Viviani is in the middle, still grinning wildly. "One more," he keeps saying. Today marks a milestone in the fire department and affirmative action, and it tickles him to death.

Word gets around fast; the telephone rings constantly, mostly for our officer, who by the looks of it is enduring a lot of ribbing. He hasn't said much to any of us, but I've worked with him before and he never said much then, so most of it isn't personal. He doesn't say much on the phone either, just reluctantly takes the handset each time, then stands mostly silent, sometimes smiling sheepishly, his bushy mustache twitching and his forearms like canoe paddles; perhaps a ladies man, but *this* is not what he had in mind. Otherwise the day is quiet—a few medical calls, a street box, one building inspection.

The full box comes in right before dinner—*fire in the building*. This is what we've wanted. We grab our coats, fling ourselves into the engine, race out the door. We don't say it explicitly but we know the pressure is on. For most, today is long awaited. Can women do this job, or are they being compensated for by the men? We pull up first. No smoke showing.

This is a disappointment. I wanted a raging fire, something that would lay to rest all the doubts people seem to have. But would anything lay to rest all the doubts? I don my air pack.

"I smell smoke," says Wendy hopefully. Sure enough, inside the building there's a thin veil hanging in the air. But where's it coming from? Soon Wendy and I are knocking on apartment doors, prying or kicking in those that aren't opened, working smoothly. Other crews begin to arrive. "Let's find this thing," Wendy says to me. "That'll really bug them."

We keep moving, sliding our hands up and down walls, sniffing adjacent rooms for smoke, knowing we need to be the ones to put water on the fire. Finally Wendy calls out, "Here!" and together we bury our axes into the plaster.

We find the fire. It only takes a small line to douse it, but it still feels good. A fire in the walls is hard to locate, and dangerous. When it's out, Wendy and I bounce up and down, making mild fun of the male boisterousness we're usually not privy to. When we exit we slap Susan on the shoulder and grin, while the other crews stare. The chief walks by.

"Good job," he says, nodding at us.

Soon I get my next assignment—to Station 4. Station 4 is a firehouse with a reputation. Usually I do not pay much attention to "reputations." However, it is with some alarm that I notice even men are taking me aside and shaking their heads. "Watch yourself there," Thomas says. Bunker shakes his burnt hand and scowls. "I like you. Don't take any shit, okay? A lot of jerks at Station 4."

I paint my helmet carefully. It offers me protection: it is ribbed for strength and curved to deflect. But what can it do against attitudes?

13.

Station 4 is wedged between crumbling buildings and shoehorned between two different worlds. On one side is one of the poorest, most crime-ridden parts of the city, where prostitutes and drug dealers crowd the street corners. A few blocks the other way, the sidewalks are clean and the buildings bright. The change is abrupt, as if a fence divides them. Emergency workers are one of the few who venture openly into both neighborhoods; otherwise there is little or no spillage, creating the bizarre feeling that one has not only turned onto the wrong block, but somehow lost consciousness and awoken into a different world.

I walk into Station 4 expectantly. I've been told to be watchful, and a part of me is, but another part believes that rumors abound in the fire department, and most are based on flimsy evidence. I have been told to think the worst of all male firefighters from the beginning, and mostly I have seen the best, so why should this station be any different? Besides, this is a busy house, and that is ultimately all I care about.

I am greeted with the same grunts and waves of a hand that any new person gets, so it is not until the middle of the morning, when another rookie pulls me aside, that I begin to worry that all the stories may be true after all. I do not know Mike well, but his best friend was in my academy class and from him he's heard that I'm all right, which is why he shifts from foot to foot now, and glances around to make sure no one sees us.

"Watch out for Todd Lane," Mike says quickly. "Last shift, at the dinner table, he said he was going to get you."

I am alarmed. "Get me? What does that mean? He doesn't even know me."

"He said he was going to cook an all-meat meal." Mike frowns, and drops his head.

At first, I'm just plain baffled. What? Ridiculous. Cooking an all-meat meal will not "get me." I don't care about food; I'm not going to starve to death in one watch.

"He deliberately switched into the cook chore today," Mike says.

"He did?" I'm still confused.

And then I realize: a firehouse meal is a bonding experience. It's a serious communion, a breaking of bread. If Todd Lane wants to exclude me, the place to do it is at dinner, and even better if he can embarrass me at the same time. It is then that the pure malice strikes me. He's volunteered for a chore that he won't get credit for, that will take him the whole day to complete, all to humiliate a person he's never even met. The magnitude of that hostility makes me go upstairs, sit in a corner, and put my face in my hands.

I consider sitting out of dinner altogether. But if I do that, I know then, that Todd Lane does "get me." The meal is sacred. To be absent is close to sacrilege. It sets you apart. The last thing I need is to be further apart.

In case Lane's ill will extends beyond the dinner, I hide my coat so no one can take it, leaving me looking ridiculous and unprepared when a call comes in. I check my turnout boots before I step into them in case someone has defecated in them, as they did to the female firefighters in New York. I speak little the rest of the day. I say nothing at all to Todd Lane.

In the dinner line, I realize that Todd Lane has done his job well. There is not a single pot that does not contain meat. The salad is full of shrimp and the beans are full of bacon. The steak is large and sullen, dripping lazily into the platter.

I do not care much about food. I have never expected others to accommodate my chosen diet. The fact that most stations have gone out of their way to make sure I have something to eat has always been a touching but extraordinary gesture, unexpected even when it occurred every shift. The irony is that right now I am so nauseous with anxiety that I could not have eaten if a vegetable garden suddenly appeared on my plate.

Years later, I would crash my paraglider against a cliff, breaking an ankle badly. When I wake up the next morning in the hospital a large hunk of chocolate cake squats on the table by my bed. A note explains that Chief Masters and Alberto had come by in the night. They had left the fire station immediately upon hearing of the accident and, armed with this massive talisman, had driven to the hospital. I am under the tender grip of Demerol and anesthesia when they arrive so they leave their loyalty and concern wrapped carefully in foil. It was enough for three and even its crumbs rolled like dimes. I am moved by the sight of this hulking piece of cake, absurdly jaunty and excessive against the swabbed, solemn backdrop of the hospital. For firefighters, food spans the place where words fail.

Todd Lane, then, knows what he is doing when he turns a meal against me. All this, and he has never met me, not even this morning; he pivoted and walked away when I came into the communications room.

I sit at the table, my plate almost empty. I fill the plate and my mouth with bread, like a wallflower who needs a drink in her hand to look occupied. I stare at a space on the table, pretending to be absorbed. I pour water. Sip. More water. Pass the bread. Pass the butter. Cut it slow, spread it slower, to make the minutes go by.

I resolve, crumbs dropping nervously on my plate, never to talk to Todd Lane at all. When he is not looking in my direction, I glance his way, taking him in, trying to understand. But what's there to understand? He seems simply to hate me.

More bread, eaten intently, as if this is all I've ever wanted in the world. Everyone has noticed by now. It's clear that whatever has happened isn't as satisfying as when it was talked about. Some of the men look uncomfortable. Some look surprised, clearly not in on the joke. I want to cover the bright white of my plate with my hand; I want to slink away.

My only other consolation is the realization that the emotion that begins to consume me—let's call it hate, why not—has already wrapped him in a brutal, suffocating embrace. My presence bothers him so much that he has arranged his whole day around it, spent hours obsessing about me, put aside everything for this. I have mattered way too much to him, even as he tries to express that I matter very little. I have the last laugh, it seems. Laughing, though, is the farthest thing from my mind.

Around this time, Alexandra lands a role on the television show *Baywatch*. *Baywatch* is a one-hour weekly drama, which features lifeguards on impeccably sunny California days making surf rescues. Frequently made fun of for its impossibly buxom females and chisel-chested males, *Baywatch* had almost been cancelled after its first season, until the television executives looked at its overseas stats, which were through the roof. A new cast was hired, my twin included, and the new *Baywatch* quickly gained a large American fan base. Now it is the most popular television program in the world. In fact, *Baywatch* is the most watched show *ever*.

Which is why I am now on the beach in Southern California, in full firefighter gear.

The photographer sent from England calls out enthusiastically, "That's right, like that. More of that, more of that." His camera is fixed to his face; his body is doing odd circles in the sand. I lean over the railing of a lifeguard tower, holding onto Alexandra by her wrists, while she dangles high off the ground, toes pointed, smile intact, red bathing suit shining in the Malibu sun. Despite this awkward position, my head is up and I am smiling too. A devil-may-care smile, I hope. Or a sexy one. I don't know which expression we are on, but there seems to be a list of them we have to get through. *Okay, give me a pout, a smile, Come hither you're saying, yeah, that's right, big eyes, this way yeah, yeah, hither....* I am glad that this is for a foreign magazine, and that no one in the fire department will see me like this, in acrobatic poses, in full gear, on the beach.

Twinship is a unique experience, but it's even more unique when your twin is famous. As *Baywatch* gets bigger, things change for me too. I am stared at—this is disconcerting—and followed—this is even more disconcerting. I am given special treatment I don't deserve: extra food is often sent to my table "on the house," employee help immediately appears at my side in supermarkets, malls, and hardware stores, and while flying to Canada I am put in first class without a word of explanation, just a small wink by the flight attendant to indicate that *she* won't tell anyone else who I am. Strangers are over-solicitous. Acquaintances are over-eager. Even when people are finally convinced of the fact that I am not the movie star (and it takes awhile) they still treat me as if I am. Soon life begins to border on the absurd. During a fire, a civilian asks my lieutenant what movie is being shot here. "This fire is real!" responds my baffled officer, to which the civilian retorts, "Then why is the *Baywatch* actress in it?" Another time, a fire drill my crew conducts at a grammar school is disrupted when kids break from the line to get my autograph, and even homeless patients claim I look familiar, much to the delight and incessant teasing of my crew.

Twins have always been gawked at. We are strange aberrations, often envied, genetic stammers not fully understood by scientists or singletons. People stare, trying to figure out who is who, combatively stating that *they* can tell us apart, as if we are trying to pull one over on them just by existing. And so we are inspected like nags at an auction—pinched, weighed, spun around, measured from fetlock to withers, teeth given the once-over. Because we are so similar, and yet not exact replicas, we are offers to the world of variations on ourselves, and people think they can eye and choose the parts and pieces they like best in each one, as if they might build a completely new person. It's a strange math—at each encounter a twin is twice what she is but only half of what she should be.

But we can withstand it. These might be fighting words, but I stand by them: twins are more self-assured than those who come into the world alone. My twin provides all the connection and comfort that we invoke from the fairy godmother, the guardian angel, the imaginary playmate, the best friend, and finally, the soul mate. We know someone will always be there for us; divorce, adultery, or plain disinterest can't destroy what we have. This makes us less lonely, and more confident, which may be why a boyfriend of Alexandra's once said in frustration that it was clear she would never really need him the way he needed her. "You have Caroline," he said, and she did not contradict him.

And now here we are, both rescuers—one on television and one in real life—and both working women enjoying different sides of the American Dream—Alexandra as a glamorous Hollywood actress and me in a non-traditional job available to hardly any other female in the world. *The Rescue Me look,* the photographer cries, lunging around us, clicking wildly. *Now tougher, tougher, yeah hands on hips, perfect, get the stance, no smiles. I'm dying, I'm drowning, great....*

On Christmas Day, I work at a station near Ocean Beach. Ocean Beach is on the northwest side of the city. It is a long, wide expanse of sand that invites slow, unguarded ambles through ankle-high water that seems deceptively manageable. In fact, the currents are strong and the waves can sweep unsuspecting waders off their feet. When the Bee-

Bop interrupts our Christmas lunch, we scramble for the Surf Rescue Truck, loaded with wet suits, kayaks and life buoys. We swing out into the crisp, sunny day.

At the beach we grab the red life buoys and scan the ocean. A park ranger points to dark dots in the water a hundred and fifty yards out; another ranger and some surfers have gotten to the man.

"He took off all his clothes at the edge. Then he went into the water and swam. Then he swam and swam and he kept on swimming. People on shore started yelling at him, but he kept on going." The ranger shrugs, as if such a thing on Christmas day is not a big surprise.

I'm a good swimmer, but I grew up near lakes, so the ocean, with its 50-degree temperatures, its big waves, and the uncomfortable clothing it requires, is new to me. I've pulled on the bulky neoprene wetsuit with some difficulty, but now I'm ready to get in the water, and as I jog to the edge, my eyes on the dots beyond the break, I get the strange sensation that I am suddenly Alexandra, suddenly a Rescue Babe, sweatless, shining, almost holy, on the way to a swift and graceful lifesaving moment.

My reverie is broken when the beach truck gets stuck in the sand and I see the currents pulling the Park Service rescuers south. There is a lot of shouting and cursing. Some firefighters try to push the truck out while others start down the beach without it. I want this rescue, so I leave the truck too, and start to run. The wetsuit makes every step graceless. I am squinting against the sun. The wind is up. When I see that the current is taking the dark dots even farther down the beach, I know for sure the fleeting *Baywatch* moment is gone.

I frequently run on this beach as a workout, which is now a godsend as I leave the others behind, and when I have passed the dots too, I cut into the ocean, slipping on my fins. I have forgotten, however, that the water here is shallow the first 30 yards or so. Unable to swim in the calf-deep water, but determined to make it out there first (First!) I shuffle and wallow and trip through the tide. I look like a huge mammal hit by a stun gun, struggling to get away.

Finally I begin to swim, and reach the exhausted park ranger and surfers. Now it's me pulling the man to shore. Nearer to the beach, more hands reach out to help. We lay the man on the sand and voices shout orders—*Get the blankets! Get the stretchers!* The man does not move, hasn't said a word throughout, as if drained by some mysterious event even larger than hypothermia. He stares at the sky and limply allows us to drop an oxygen mask on him and roll him onto a board. The ranger, breathless from his part in the rescue, takes off his cap and runs a stiff hand through his hair.

"Poor bastard didn't even struggle when we got to him. He just stopped swimming and tried to sink."

The man's wide, detached silence continues. From the looks of it, he wants not just to die, but to disintegrate slowly, to swim while feeling drops off into the cold, first the fingers, then the face, then the legs. Swim until he can feel nothing and then slowly sink. It is a gentle way to die, I suppose, but there is something about his passionless agony that seems even more terrible than a gunshot wound or an intentional overdose.

But I am exhilarated. A surf rescue!

Even when I realize, as I walk away, that I have put my wetsuit on backwards.

Meanwhile, Station 4 keeps me busy, and soon the potential that something *can* happen is almost as exciting as the happening itself. When the Bee-Bop goes off, I realize that I have been waiting for it. We jump onto the rig and careen into the dirty streets of the poor neighborhood. The sirens whine, the lights flash and, now that "something" has happened, the call opens up wide with possible adventure.

I respect the crew I work with, but it's never comfortable at Station 4. I don't care—I'll take polite exclusion because the station is busy. I don't see Todd Lane after that first encounter, except in distant passing. Mostly I keep to myself. As long as the calls keep coming in, making this job worthwhile, I can do that.

When Jackie brings harassment charges against Captain John Wills I know she is not lying or imagining things. The case throws the department into a tizzy and me, in particular, into a depression.

Jackie is a friend of mine. I want to protect her, but I also want to assimilate. Secretly, I hope that I will not have to testify on her behalf. *Please, please, please.* This weakness surprises and embarrasses me; I assumed that I would always willingly stand up for a friend.

Captain Wills looks for a woman to testify as a character witness. I am relieved that I do not know him and will not be asked. Meanwhile, Jackie stops speaking to anyone. She takes time off for stress. She does not return my phone calls.

"Of course this crap happens," another classmate, Carl, says to me. Carl is a burly white man who told some of his crew members that he was looking for a house to buy for his family. He mentioned an area near the almost exclusively black Hunter's Point neighborhood. One of the lieutenants listening leaned forward.

"It is bad enough we have to work with them," he said. "Why do you want to live with them too?"

Carl stared at the lieutenant.

"Just so you know, I am *married* to one of them." That ended the conversation.

When Carl tells me this story he does not seem surprised or particularly outraged, as if his years in an interracial marriage have long shown him the worst in people.

I attend the fire department hearing on the Wills case. The meeting room is packed; many of the top brass and the department administrators are present. Off-duty firefighters and Union leaders whisper among themselves.

Jackie, usually animated, is slack-faced. When she takes the stand, her words are slow and precise, her inflections flat and emotionless. I am shocked by the change in her. She relates in a low voice how Captain Wills mimicked Hymie the Clown behind her back. Hymie the Clown is a character on Saturday Night Live, where he is presented as a black clown prone to violence. Wills, in his imitation, stood behind her and pretended to hit her. Other comments were made, one on the size of her buttocks. One after another, each of the white firefighters present that day say that they do not remember this Hymie the Clown act, nor any of the other comments Wills is alleged to have made throughout the shift. Jackie, the lone black and the lone woman, is outnumbered.

This sudden affliction of amnesia does not help Captain Wills. He is suspended. Jackie does not return to work for a long time.

14.

On the day of the Oakland fire, I am working. It is a normal day for Station 4. It seems to be a normal day for Oakland, a large city within view across the bay, as firefighters there respond to what they think is a small, successfully extinguished grass fire. They throw some more water on it, and go back to the station.

Unfortunately, embers remain.

By noon a wildfire is out of control in the exclusive Oakland hills. Mansions and large housing complexes heave and sigh once or twice before being engulfed. The flames jump Highway 24. A battalion chief dies. Part wildfire, part structure fire, part hell-on-earth, the crews are overwhelmed. Oakland frantically radios surrounding cities for assistance.

San Francisco sends engines immediately, but my crew is not one of them. Nevertheless, we pace the communications floor, keeping an eye on the teletype, trying to understand the scope of the disaster. We switch frantically between television channels as reporters on scene wipe their eyes from the smoke and scream into their microphones, and the cameras swing around to show exploding trees, houses in flames, and evacuating cars. Mutual aid streams toward Oakland from all over the state, and volunteers start showing up at the station to grab their go-bags and fire gear.

As the fire gets bigger and the sky blacker, and more off-duty fire-fighters pour into the station to pick up equipment, I get more and more depressed. I stare forlornly at the flying saucer of smoke that now creeps toward us from across the bay, while Richard leans over yet another drunk sleeping on the curb.

"Looks like we're going to miss all the fun," he says with a chuckle. He likes to joke. But I'm in no mood.

"Maybe it'll go until tomorrow," I say sadly. I use the word "go" so I don't have to say "burn", which is what I really mean. It's embarrassing to want the devastation to last until I am free to volunteer, but it's true. Anyway, Richard understands. He loves to fight fires. He's built like Atlas, huge lats, biceps as big as steaks, a tapered waist. African American, he's liked by everyone for his genial nature, and admired for his strength. He laughs at me again, but now he too looks up at the sky a little bitterly. With hundreds of structures already burned, this is the biggest firestorm we've ever seen, and we're going to miss it.

By dinnertime the ash fall is heavy, smoke chokes the streets outside, and there are warnings to watch for fire in San Francisco. We remain glued to the television. It is a particularly despondent feeling, to be so far from the action, and we all share it. The few jokes told around the table are made wanly and greeted with bitter grunts.

Most of the San Francisco firefighters are posted at the Claremont Hotel, which is the second biggest wooden structure in the United States. There is fear that if the Claremont burns it may set all of downtown Berkeley on fire. But San Francisco stops it there, and soon the teams will return home with big stories of heroism and adventure.

The statistics from the Firestorm, as the media begins to call it, tell a story of how mighty fire is. Emergency beacons melt, cars detonate, fifty houses on one street all burn at the same time. In all, 3,469 living units are destroyed, 2,843 of them single-family homes. Five hundred twenty acres burned. A 5.2 miles fire perimeter. Twenty-five deaths.

I cheer up momentarily when I am told that Tess, in full uniform, was stopped by a reserve police officer on the lookout for looters. The police officer demanded identification, but she had none, as her mutual aid team had only minutes to get ready. She was in full turnout gear, of course, but in the eyes of the police officer this was not proof that she was a firefighter, because after all she was a woman, and she probably stole it from her boyfriend. She was indignant; he arrested her for "impersonating a firefighter." Ignoring her outrage, he hand-cuffed her and threw her into the back of his police car. A surprised fire chief identified her after she convinced the police officer to drive to where the San Francisco Fire department was making a stand. "Get out, bitch," the police officer said.

I have stayed clear of Tess ever since her withdrawn handshake and her laugh at my expense. But now I feel sorry for her. All her years in the fire department has not yet changed the outside world.

Meanwhile in every firehouse stories circulate about the Firestorm, the flames bigger and hotter with each retelling. I sulk quietly.

The warehouse fire comes in around midnight. It's a real worker when we arrive, and since the warehouse is full of tea, a sweet, floral smell fills the air. I run into Patricia near a big line. She says that she and her crew had tried an interior attack but had been forced to retreat. The stairs they were on started to collapse, she said, and the roof began to fall in. She repeats that they almost "lost it" and there is amazement in her voice and a smile on her face.

From then on we are ordered to surround and drown, which is mostly boring, except it gives you a chance to stare, hypnotized, at the flames. For a few hours I hold various hoses, but soon I take my turn on the top of the aerial ladder.

The smoke is so thick, it's like climbing into a cloud on my way to heaven. The ladder shakes with each step. It's best not to look down in order to keep your stomach in check, but I do anyway and see the city spread below in small, precise lights. The warehouse, its flames leaping through the roof, recedes. When I reach the top—80 feet up—I signal for water.

Every now and then directions from the intercom tell me where to direct the nozzle stream. Otherwise, I am cut off from the world below. I look at the view, breathless, and then suddenly there will be nothing—no city lights, no burning warehouse, not even a ladder that I'm standing on—as steam and smoke wafts up, whites everything out, then opens again. Underneath me, the three-story warehouse refuses to surrender, and finally the cement walls split in the heat, the sound like sudden shots from a gun. After an hour I am soaking wet, but I don't want to come down. The air is sweet with tea. I'm alone; it's strangely peaceful, strangely beautiful.

Finally, I'm shivering too much. I descend reluctantly into the pungent air. When I reach the turntable I nod at the firefighter waiting there to go up and take my place above the world, and dawn breaks over the smoldering building.

15.

One foot in front of the other, slowly, carefully. Deep breath. Hands out as if grasping thin air. Not thin air exactly, but close enough: only a cartilage of wire on each side of me. The wind picks up now, and I think that if I stop I might get blown off. More steps, slowly, carefully. Beneath my feet, a three foot diameter cable. Below that, nothing for 746 feet.

If this was a skyscraper, I would be the window washer outside the 63rd floor. But it's not a skyscraper, it's the Golden Gate bridge. More accurately, it's the suspension cable above the bridge that leads up to the north tower. I say that because accuracy seems absurdly important right now, as does the difference between the cable and the bridge itself. The bridge—I see this from my vantage point now with some sadness—is wide, sturdy, safe and inviting. The narrow cable I'm walking on is flimsy and, frankly, terrifying.

Now that I've made the mistake of looking down, I might as well keep looking. I watch a car pass by with nary a care, shrunk to the size of my fingernail. The ocean hits a cliff and the surf peels into white, blinking in the dark. It is as if the earth unzips a layer momentarily, and then zips it back up. I hear the waves break too, but from so high up it sounds only like a whisper.

To the left is the city. Always a beautiful skyline, tonight it is framed by the long cables of the easterly suspension so that it stands out like a prized painting. In the foreground is Alcatraz Island, once a notorious prison, now lit to look like a small castle. Behind that is the long spidery stretch of the Bay Bridge. Why didn't we pick that bridge to climb, I wonder. It is a squat bridge with none of the high, dizzying aspects of the Golden Gate.

Why am I up here? It is the third time I ask myself. Behind me are four other slim, dark silhouettes, moving slowly, bent in concentration like monks. At this point the question is simply rhetorical; turning around and going back down would be as bad as continuing up. The simple answer is that we're here because someone suggests it, and at the time it sounds interesting and easy. It is Ellie's idea. *Come on, it'll be fun, it'll be crazy, what the hell.* She has done it once, a year before, with her boyfriend and some of his friends, but this time she wants only girls and gathers her team. First, Beth, long time rafting teammate and close friend of mine, then me, and Janet, a mountain climber. I ask Melea, my girlfriend, to come too. "You don't have to if you don't want," I say off-handedly, which does the trick. Melea is good to have around, because she's calm, sensible. If she's agreed to our adventure, it can't be that stupid.

My hands are getting cold. The cable rears up now at a sharper angle; I walk on my toes to stay balanced. Behind me I can hear Ellie singing snatches of Waltzing Mathilda, some words coming intermittently toward me, the others flung into the wind. Melea is quiet, and so is Beth. Farther behind is Jane, who wears full climbing gear. She slides a carabiner along one side of her, unhooking every now and then to get past a cross wire. All five of us have climbed before, but only Jane decides to use her gear. She's probably the smart one, but the rest of us have weighed our options and decide that the psychological comfort of having a grip in the cable at all time trumps the hooking and unhooking of the climbing equipment. Below us, the cars have become tiny.

If I ever come up here again, I remind myself, it won't be like this, black-clad and secretive, whispering. I'll be here in a fire coat and a helmet. I'll be official, sent with my new crew, probably to stop a jumper (this bridge is famous for both its color and its suicides) or help a trapped bridge worker. This is because I've just gotten a permanent spot on the rig I've wanted for a long time: Rescue Squad 2.

There are fire engines and there are fire trucks. In San Francisco there are also two specialized teams, called Rescue Squads. Rescue Squads do just that: rescue, of all types. So it wouldn't be too crazy to be back here one day in the future, walking up this cable to talk down a stupid yahoo who thinks it's fun and character-building to climb to the top of the Golden Gate Bridge with her equally stupid, yahoo friends.

Squad members are called Squaaaadieeeeees by other fire crews, part Tarzan yell, part whine, a teasing reminder that for all the glamour of being on a Rescue Squad, don't go getting too big for your britches. "Here come the white scarves," is another common refrain, a reference to World War I flying aces, and the fact that the Squad swoops in with their equipment and expertise and then swoops out, leaving the mess of overhaul and cleanup to everyone else.

The truth is, not a lot of people want to be on the Squad. It's busy, and you have to take a lot of classes to qualify. I must get my scuba dive search and rescue certificate, my coast guard boat driving license, my tunnel rescue certification, a confined space certification, my surf rescue certification, my hazardous materials certification, my rappelling and climbing skills tuned up and my Heavy Rescue 1 certification. It's a pain, but it's worth it in the end; the Rescue Squads get the best, most exciting, calls in the whole city.

The official color of the Golden Gate Bridge is not golden. It is "international orange," the color judged to be the easiest to see in fog (next to black and white checkers, which is what the Coast Guard originally argued for), and there is some debate before we start climbing about what color clothing to wear. We dig in our closets for international orange possibilities. Black, an easier color to find, is our eventual choice. We're sorority sisters, on a hazing routine, someone suggests. Okay, we agree, that's our story, as if sorority sisters will get some sort of break if caught.

The plan is to get to the bridge at midnight, so we decide to see the late show of Sylvester Stallone's climbing movie *Cliffhanger*, to pass the time and psyche us up. The choice is a mistake; in the first scene a climber is pitched into a chasm after the unlikely mechanical failure of a buckle. Now we are here, and it runs through my mind that the wires I hold onto could snap, the cable I walk on could sever, the bridge itself collapse.

The red light is just ahead. Ellie has warned us about this; she claims that it's a video camera and we should avert our faces and duck by. From my vantage point I can see that there is nowhere to "duck" unless we execute some strange maneuver that would entail hanging from the underside of our already precarious foothold. I stop and slowly turn to confer with the group. I'm momentarily dizzy—I'm looking down again, at four dark shapes and the cable that falls away like an unfurling rope.

This is the first time women have made permanent spots on a Rescue Squad: I on Rescue 2 and Mimi on the other rig, Rescue 1. The department seems to go into collective shock over it—women on the Squad! Mimi belonged to the second class of women in, and she's aggressive and competent. A construction worker before she was a firefighter, she reminds me of a power tool—solidly built, strong. She doesn't speak much; she rarely says a word to me, though I see her sometimes at my gym where she easily presses almost twice my body weight. Her boyfriend is another firefighter, and rumor has it he has another girlfriend, a "biker chick" known to carry a knife and a bad temper, though I imagine that Mimi could easily defend herself if it came down to it. Mimi did speak a full sentence to me once. I had trouble starting a saw during a drill. She walked over soundlessly, waved me aside wordlessly, pulled the cord contemptuously and the engine roared to life so fast it sounded as if it was trying to back away from her.

"Put your foot here," she said suddenly, without looking at me. "And your left hand, not your right, on the cord. Now you're right over it—see? And it'll pull straight and nicely."

A few months later, a saw needed to open a roof on a fire building wouldn't start. What the hell, I thought, and stepped up to try. To my surprise and everyone else's—except perhaps Mimi's if she had been there—it started immediately.

We are still contemplating the red light, and I can see that the cable now gleams with a thick dusting of dew. We decide to run. "Run" is a relative term when you are on a slick suspension cable and the wind is blowing and anxiety and adrenalin is forcing a strange mix of chemicals into your legs, which are about to lock up. But we try, each moving as fast as possible past the video camera, stiff-legged and stiff-armed, Frankensteinesque in our hurry.

Rescues on the local bridges are not uncommon. A few years ago, Rescue 1 pulled a jumper off of the Bay Bridge. The man had climbed over the railing to jump and then lost his nerve. Squaddies rappelled to him and brought him back up. Once a firefighter on the way to work saw a man lean over the side of the Golden Gate Bridge and disappear. The firefighter jumped out of his car and climbed out after him. The man was sitting on a girder getting up the guts to jump while the off-duty firefighter shimmied towards him. They sat talking high over the bay, the large ribs of the mammoth structure above them. Perhaps they talked about beer and football and the meaning of life. Eventually, the suicidal man changed his mind, and both climbed back up onto the walkway.

We are near the top now. The cable rears to meet the tower so steeply that my hands seem to be at eye level. I walk on my tiptoes to accommodate the angle and pull myself along the last ten yards, like someone infirm would do up a staircase. Why do we do these silly things? But even as I ask myself one last time, everything narrows to just this step, then that one, then that one. My petty worries stay back, I feel fully present. I wade through heightened emotions in no particular order: anxiety, wonder, joy, regret, and back to anxiety again. This is why, of course. Danger brings with it beauty, exhilaration, and a sense that if we can take this next step, then we can do anything.

The top is bathed in spotlights. Above is that purple-ish sky peculiar to cloudy city nights. The shadow of the bridge is strewn across it, reflected in long dark lines. It's a strange and eerie sight, beautiful and scary. And then suddenly it is there. The top! The pinnacle! The zenith! I shimmy from the suspension, and drop down onto the damp, steel surface. I lie there for a moment, arms outstretched as if I've been stranded at sea and have just found shore. I stare at the rivulets that the braided wire has left in my palm and I know what Patricia tells me is true. "You're such an idiot," I say to myself, grinning, wincing, grinning. Then slowly I sit up, and wait for Melea and the others.

16.

On a cool day, you can catch the faint smell of ash and antiseptic. The mild stink of wet neoprene clings to the scuba tanks in the corner. A sting of rubbing alcohol hits the nose. Perhaps the timid hint of blood.

Today, it has rained so we have tracked crooked lines of mud on the metal floor. Stacks of ropes in blue bags take up the left top shelves like large sleeping cats. Helmets to one side. Then the gibs, the pulleys, the carabiners. Below are the bulky trauma bags, soft and heavy with tape and bandages and face masks. Bottles of distilled water stand like stout soldiers.

On the right are the wetsuits, folded and piled on top of each other. The fins and masks. The thick gloves and hoods. Sometimes, if the driver takes a corner too fast, a fin flies out at you. Other things have fallen on me too—the defibrillator, the burn kit, a flashlight. I sometimes wonder how they will find me if we ever have an accident—smothered, decapitated, gashed in a thousand places—brutally, spectacularly killed by the vast and varied equipment that we use to rescue people.

This is Rescue 2. Sometimes it is simply called *the rig*, as are most of the other vehicles of the San Francisco Fire Department. *What rig are you on today?* you might be asked. *That rig*, you say. You point, because there are many rigs and they are all red and seem larger than life. *That rig.*

Alberto stands near the hazardous material clothing cabinets. He runs a bakery on his off days; perhaps this accounts for the way he slowly puts his helmet on and carefully cinches up his belt. Even in the midst of chaos, he is thoughtful and centered. It is as if fighting a fire is somehow like baking bread and he is used to it: the heat, the stress, the firm grip on the axe handle is not much different than the rolling pin. He has a thick black moustache and short black hair. He assures me that once he had a beard and long hair, but it is hard to believe.

There are only two windows in the rig, and they are small and impossible to see out of, so there is the odd sensation of traveling wildly and fast, but with very little sense of where one is heading. Time does not seem to move forward, but from side to side in angular, jerky movements.

Even if Alberto and I cannot see where we're going, we recognize the roll and sway of the streets in our dispatch area. I hear the engine accelerate down wide South Van Ness Avenue. In narrow alleys, with double parked cars and errant garbage cans, we slow down. But not much. This is the Mission District, full of old wooden houses and crowded, noisy intersections.

For many years, Rescue Squad 2 was stationed in the city's wealthy Pacific Heights area, and there weren't many calls. Rescue 1, on the other hand, was posted in one of the most crime-ridden parts of San Francisco, and they were busy all the time. As a result, they called themselves The Squad. They called Rescue 2 the Other Squad, or in kinder moments the U-Turn Squad, because Rescue 2 was often cancelled from the emergency while still on its way.

A few years ago, Rescue 2 was quietly removed from the mansions of Pacific Heights and placed in its new home at Station 64. Here, there is more work. The Mission District is crowded and poor. Crack and heroin are the drugs of choice. Molotov cocktails or .22s are the weapons of choice, sometimes machetes. Fires start easily in the crowded, rundown wood houses. Rescue 2 is no longer a U-turn rig.

The brakes hiss and catch. We jump out, momentarily disoriented, but we smell the smoke immediately. The air packs are lifted from their compartment and held high above our heads so that they drop onto our backs easily. It is a small silent game here, though Alberto doesn't notice. He is slow and careful in his movements and not in any race. But the rest of us want to be the first with the air pack on, the first to get to the building.

Miller plays this game grimly. He would hate to get beaten by a woman. He does not talk to me, but if he did he might well say that he is glad that he is not my partner today. Miller hates to work with a woman. Second to that probably comes working with a baker. Miller himself is short and pudgy, soft enough to look like a girl from behind, so sometimes I'm curious about his macho swagger, his silent vehemence, but not now. The only thing that matters now is the fire.

Someone is being carried out and laid on the sidewalk. The smoke is black and angry and pours out of the side windows. An engine hose runs up the steps and into the blackness.

The Rescue Squad goes in without water, because our purpose is to rescue, not to put the fire out. Sometimes it seems crazy, to run in without water. But only when someone asks me about it—*how can you go in like that, without protection, without water*—do I take a minute and think about it, and it does seem crazy. But then I forget about it. It is not something you can ponder too much.

"Does anyone else live over there?" I ask the neighbor as Alberto and I charge through his house. He stammers and shakes, overwhelmed by the sight of these helmeted, clanging, sooty firefighters running on his tan carpet, through his neat hallway. In the garden I get ready to jump the back fence to gain access to the rear entrance of the burning building. I have over fifty pounds of gear on, but I have gotten over a lot of fences. The neighbor has clung to us, followed us past his flower vases and through his geraniums. Now he waves me off the fence hurriedly, worriedly, and points to a missing plank we can squeeze through.

At the house I turn to kick in the back door. I miss the wood and my foot crashes through the pane glass. I bend and unlock the door from the inside, and make a mental note to practice my aim.

We kneel, knocking our helmets back. We fit our air masks against our faces, and the respirator kicks in. We plunge forward.

Inside it is pitch black. Tables, clocks, a phone, books, a couch. All these things shift in and out of sight, materializing through touch and the weak, unreliable light of my flashlight. But I am looking for something else: a hand, the flower print of a dress, the curve of a chin. Anything can start to look like these, so I must not let my mind jog ahead into the smoke. Instead, each moment must be allowed to sit and reveal what it will in its own time. Nothing can be missed. It is an odd discipline for a firefighter intent on rushing ahead to divert the future. I listen to the surf of my breath to keep me centered—in, out, and then it swirls within the closed mask like the rush of a wave.

We break windows to ventilate the smoke and heat. I crawl over chairs, and around a side table. A stereo appears in the blackness only when my face mask is pressed close to it. We pat the floor and make wide sweeps with our hands as if to smooth bedsheets; this is the only way to be sure we don't miss a body in the dark. As we round a corner on our knees, it grows suddenly hot and there is the blur of orange through the smoke.

On cue there is the sound of water. The smoke clears fast now. To the left a window is broken and through it I can see dusk gently outlining the skyscrapers of downtown. To the right is the Bay Bridge. The lights that line the span are beginning to turn on, making the water below it purple. A tanker with a red belly seems to shine momentarily, and then loses the last rays of the day.

"They were goddamn lucky," Joe says and his silhouette gestures to Alberto and me. The hiss of steam and the loud voices of men take up the space where the silence and the thick, hot darkness had once been.

We head back to the rig, walking slowly to let the adrenalin seep back from the crevices and corners of our bodies. The clatter of broken wood and the soft, whooshing sound of wet, burnt belongings thrown on concrete begin their familiar rhythm behind me. In some ways this is the most heartbreaking part, more so even than the burning house. The pieces of someone's life are thrown in misshapen black heaps on the curb, then separated with the pick of a stranger's axe, and nonchalantly hosed down.

There is a moment of my own I want to hold onto. It is the deep, swaying continuum between me and my crew, as if our turnout coats and helmets were attached by some invisible thread. It was a good fire and we have done a good job together. Even Miller cannot ruin this camaraderie. Then the moment is over, and I hear the long, thin wail of the owner as the last of the belongings are soaked down with the hose.

"See ya at the Big One," someone from another crew says as he walks by on his way back to his rig. "Yeah," laughs Joe, and the man laughs back.

The Mission District is named for the church that stands on its edge, Mission Dolores, the oldest structure in the city and one of 21 missions established by Franciscan Jesuits, who used it to convert the local Costanoan tribe back in 1776. San Francisco as we know it grew outward from here, but in the process seemed to leave the mission and the old district behind. Now the neighborhood's shabby Victorian houses, dense population and grimy streets overshadow the proud heritage. But it makes Rescue 2 a busy, adventurous assignment.

The old shift talks about the calls they had over the past twenty-four hours as the new shift wanders in and prepares for the day. Cabinets slam. Sports pages are unfurled and cracked loudly. Someone polishes his boots in rhythmic arcs. From the television there is the drone of newscasters. The clink of coffee cups. Loud voices, getting louder.

The coffee is weak as usual, but I pour a cup anyway. It is a habit from four years ago, back when Johnny poured me my first cup. As I sip it, I listen to the clangor around me. It is almost eight o'clock in the morning. Yesterday's game is debated, dissected, debunked. With hindsight, everyone throws, passes, strategizes differently and better. I sit down next to Tim and Hal, tight in conversation about the 49ers. I am amazed at their intensity and seriousness as they hunch over each play, as if they are speaking about death or family problems. Tim has long hair pinned untidily behind his head. One hand is on his suspenders, which he pulls when making a point.

The fire from our last shift is mentioned, but only briefly.

"Did the person who was carried out and laid on the sidewalk die?"

"I don't think so," someone says. Shrugs, nods. We are privy to small sentences of other people's lives, their intimate, tragic moments, but not the whole story. For us, it ends at the sidewalk or at the emergency room door.

"A drill today, so don't get too comfortable," Joe says as he walks by. He walks at a slant, leaning forward and a little sideways as if to compensate for some gravitational pull no one else feels. It's his bad back, and we know this, but people speak to him with their feet wide and their arms crossed, as if whatever force is pulling on him might suddenly affect them as well.

I like Joe. He's fair, and I will go so far as to say he respects me, though we've never had a conversation about it. He's also calm in an emergency, not like some officers whose voices rise in pitch during a fire, and who move with jerky indecision. Not Joe. He is not tall or big, but most of us would rather be with him in a burning building than anyone else. He is a great example of how brute size and strength is not in and of itself vital—smarts and bravery make a great firefighter. If Joe does not have the strength to throw a big victim on his shoulder, he will simply wrap webbing under the man's arms and drag him.

Joe is back with a bowl of ice cream. "Climbing drill or scuba drill?" he asks.

But before the drill, or anything else, the station must be cleaned. The station is huge. It is home to as many as twenty of us each twenty-four-hour shift. We clean it every day, which at first seems excessive. But when I remember the news article that I read that said that most dust is made up of skin particles, I know that it would not take long to cover the desks and floors with a thin, snowy layer of exfoliation. With the fire department divided into three shifts, there are sixty people who flake quietly around this three-story building.

My assignment for the morning cleanup is to sweep and mop the apparatus floor. I like the apparatus floor, where all the rigs park in silent repose. There is a wide quiet in this huge hangar, and a solemn order. The lockers are lined neatly along the walls. Boxes of supplies are stacked tightly on each other. Each rescue vehicle stretches out next to another and offers its own precise geometry: the square Rescue Squad, the long thin truck, the one short, lithe engine, the short chief's "buggy." As if to break up this linear harmony, brass poles drop here and there, providing quick access from the dormitory above. The apparatus floor is a model of quiet and calm now, but we all know that's tenuous. At any moment the emergency tone will echo across the tiled floor and high ceilings, shattering the silence and order. Engines will roar to life. Shards of red and white lights will roll across opening doors. The rigs will wail, then uncoil and leap out into the city, heading to the emergency. Once we're gone, the apparatus doors will lower and the calm will descend again, until we return, at which time the doors will open, the rigs will back in and we will wait for the next emergency.

It is the eternal illusion that chaos can be managed that gives the apparatus floor some of its magic, but mostly it is the chaos itself, the explosion of sound and light and movement, which leaves everyone spellbound.

I bring the mop down on the floor, and through the various oil patches, ashen boot marks and mud flecks that are more eloquent than words about the daily life here. Outside, a chainsaw starts, and horns are honked. My neatly pressed pant legs lose part of their sharp crease as I splash hot soapy water on the floors and myself. By the end of the shift my uniform will resemble the floor, the day's adventures spilling across in butter marks, grease, blood drops, sweat stains and ash.

Alberto walks up to help me finish. He pauses at the large apparatus door, open to the day. It is a typical morning in San Francisco. The fog was thick and heavy for a while, but now it rolls away. From the front of the fire station, where we look towards the hills and beyond, to the ocean, it pulls itself back like a thick horse's neck, wisps fanning out like a white mane. You cannot see the ocean but you can feel it, a cold thick wind that smells like fish.

Alberto strokes his black moustache and I let my fingers tap the seam of each pant leg. As the fog recedes further, the light takes on a silvery glow, and throws streaks of sunlight through the sky. Someone turns the radio on in the workroom. The hulking apparatus floor sends the sounds of the football game floating past us and into the street. I shift and take a step away. Alberto looks down at the asphalt and kicks softly with one boot. We are wary of beautiful things. Perhaps we think that they will make us soft. We turn and walk in.

"We're getting a fire today," Alberto says, as we head to the kitchen.

"Sure," I say.

Alberto pushes open the door to the communications room and we walk in. "No, really. I can feel it." Alberto turns to Miller. "I can feel it, a busy day. It's the way the back of my throat feels. It always knows."

"That's thirst," I say, sitting down at the kitchen table. Miller says nothing. He fishes one hand into a round tin of chewing tobacco and chops at the center of the sports page with the other.

Joe approaches and slaps at his newspaper. "Miller, you're off to defibrillator class. Nick will take your place until you get back."

Squad members are constantly going to class. There are numerous re-certifications, protocols, and newfangled equipment on which we have to be up to date. Our latest is a medical device modeled after a toilet plunger. It is used on chest compressions during cardio-pulmonary resuscitation. After a man collapsed from a massive heart attack, his son saved his life by using a real toilet plunger. Doctors, amazed at the man's recovery, found that the suction ability of the toilet plunger drew much more blood into the heart than ordinary CPR. Now we have modified toilet plungers on some of the rigs on a trial basis.

This is only the latest effort to substitute for the work of the heart, and it is no less comical than earlier ones. In the 18th century I would have thrown the patient over a horse and clucked it to a trot. Some people built fires on the chests of dead people, hoping to connect with some inner fire of life. Later, the Navy hung a still warm body on a barrel and rolled it back and forth.

"And we've got to have a drill," Joe adds. "Scuba or climbing. You guys pick."

"Nick wants to shake for it," Nick says. He runs a hand through his short hair and grins. He speaks about himself in the third person loudly and with his whole body, thrusting his hips out and sitting back on his heels to take up more space. His eyes never stop moving, giving the impression that he's not quite listening, and constantly looking for something else.

"Nick's up for a dive on such a beautiful day," he says.

None of us care, but we like to shake. The dice roll around like small hiccups in the brown cup.

Before Nick can continue a monologue, the Bee-Bop begins. We recognize it instinctively, stopping before we consciously know why, realizing we have been waiting for it all along. Sometimes in department stores, the tone that signals a sale will go off and it is not until the voice begins *Smart shoppers, in aisle 5...* that I realize my arms are stiff, my breathing has stopped, and I feel as if I am about to take off running.

Fire in the building, bellows the loudspeaker.

My coat is still damp from the fire the shift before. I pull it on as we hurtle around a corner. Its grip is cold and heavy on my arms. My helmet slides out of reach on the shelf and I wait until we turn the other way, which we do with a squeal and a blast of the air horn. I catch my helmet mid-slide, and flip it on my head, moving to avoid Nick. He is flailing his arms to stay balanced. He is saying something, as usual.

The building is old and brown, and crowded with windows that look lopsided. These are the buildings to watch out for, the cheap hotels that have escaped newer safety laws. They have empty hose boxes on each floor—their hoses recently pawned by heroin addicts. Their stairways are narrow, their hallways a maze, and the rooms are crowded with garbage and people sliding into their highs. These buildings are lonely and sad; they are also lethal. Now, people stream out of the narrow doorway. I smell something but I see no smoke.

"No smoke," Nick says.

We pound up the stairs, driven by adrenalin. I am third behind Joe and Nick, because I fiddled too long with the air pack, which lately has been catching on my right shoulder. I swear under my breath.

On the first floor people point up, skinny fingers poking the air; I have no time to notice their faces. The stairwell is steep. Then I see the smoke. But it is not thick, or heavy. It fills the hall with a gauzy haze. A police officer stands at a doorway, an extinguisher in his hand. We run into the room.

A man is curled in the corner, a dark shadow except for a sprinkle of white from the fire extinguisher. Then I see the orange embers on his shirt, the way it hangs from his body in shreds.

Nick is a paramedic. The horror does not slow his hands. Instantly, fingers find the neck.

"Jesus Christ, he's got a pulse," he says. He pats the embers furiously, and then he pulls the man away from the wall and lays him down to begin emergency treatment.

The whole body is burned.

The man does not lie down, but remains curiously tangled in himself. His arms reach forward, rigid. His hands are stumps, the fingers gone. I grab his forearms to pull them to his sides, but they are stiff, unmoving, and I let go with a gasp. Joe opens the oxygen bag and quickly pulls out the tank. In a daze, I pick up the mask. Nick is pale and keeps saying *Jesus Christ, Jesus Fucking Christ* until Joe tells him sharply to shut up.

It is impossible to tell how old the man is. I think he is African-American until his pants are cut away. Only his legs are not burned; they are pale and thin. Everything else is charred and flaking like the side of an old building. I have the oxygen mask so I must now look at his face.

He has no face. It is as if it blurred and then sank into itself. Eyes welded shut, nose gone, mouth a small hole that he cannot move. I have an oral airway in my hand—a small plastic device to keep the tongue from blocking the throat—but I think I might tear a long gash if I try to get it into the mouth. I have a sudden vision of all the skin sliding away, revealing only a grinning skull.

"It'll fit," Joe says as if reading my mind. He takes the oral airway from me and twists and pushes. He is right. It is in place and the skin is still intact. I let my breath out, unaware I had even held it in. I place the mask on the faceless face and reach down to get a seal. I do not look down as I make contact, but whisper to myself, *please.* I don't know who I am talking to or what I mean, but it is enough. My hand is there and this strange non-face has not collapsed, and it does not feel soft or gooey or as if it will break apart under me. I press the first few liters of oxygen into his lungs. His arms, seared into place, reach up past my shoulder. He cannot speak, but his body says enough; he is locked in an agonizing beseechment.

The engine crew is at the stairwell, breathing heavily, the hose in their hand. Joe waves them back. Off to the side I see the truck crew, holding axes and ceiling hooks like limbs askew. They are silent.

"Are you sure you got a pulse?" I ask Nick.

"Fucking positive," he almost screams, tearing at the clothes with scissors.

I am surprised. Nick, losing it? Nick the paramedic who once proudly ran down his list of medical experience to me: the 12-year-old girl who had been sodomized; a mother shot by her son; legless, headless humans, all of which accounted for why he was so hard, *so unfeeling*. "That is why Nick's so fucking fucked up," he had said, his eyes darting about, laughing in that weird way of his.

Then the man's legs move. They scrape across the floor as the legs of an insect half-stepped-on might. They trace a jerky circle, and the effort is immense. He is trying to move other parts of himself, but they will not budge. He is cemented in place by his burns. Everything is seared closed.

A noise comes from his throat.

I wonder what he is thinking. Locked in darkness with only agonizing pain and great heat—*this is hell*, his mind must be screaming. I want to lean in and say *no, this is not hell, you are burned, someone set you on fire, and I am the firefighter in charge of your breathing, so stay calm, maybe go to sleep, and the ambulance will be here soon*, but it sounds dumb, it sounds corny, so I say nothing and keep clenching my teeth and squeezing the bag. I remember the old woman so long ago, whom I could not comfort either, and I wonder, *what the hell have I learned?* Joe asks me if I want a break and I shake my head.

"Where is the fucking ambulance?" Nick shouts. Joe gets on the radio, and the hum of his voice takes my attention away from the noise in the man's throat.

Miller stands by the banister. He stares, probably wishing that he had left on time for his medical class. I can tell by the way his jaw is held that he has chew in and has not spit in awhile. He has forgotten all about it and a brown line seeps from the curve of his mouth. I lean towards the burned man.

"The ambulance is coming soon," I begin quietly. "Real soon." I squeeze the bag into that melted face. "You've been burned, and we're the fire department, so just relax. The ambulance will be here soon. Promise." I close my eyes and concentrate on the rhythmic squeal of the rubber bag.

The police hold up a bottle of vodka, and whisper among themselves. This is the ignition fuel, they say, and shake their heads. The firefighters don't say much at all; we see ourselves in the twisted man on the floor. The possibility of burning alive is very real to each of us, something so real that we don't even let ourselves think about it except in nightmares. Nick swears under his breath again. "Nick hates this, man, just fucking hates this," he murmurs.

The engine crew parts and two paramedics push through. Nick gives a quick report. "He was on fire next to the window. Trying to jump out I think," he says, voice tight, "Partial thickness burns all down his back and buttocks. You see the goddamn face. The whole chest. It's bad."

The woman paramedic works fast. She puts her bag down. Her eyes flicker over the body, shock registering for a moment before the usual defenses are mustered, then her face falls slack and expressionless. "Board," she says. "Load and go. No messing around."

Her partner throws out the burn sheets; hands wrap the man in it. Faceless, voiceless, bodiless, he is given shape and form by our imaginations only, embodying our worst fears. We describe it in culinary terms, but that is only to hide how unpalatable, how unfathomable, it really is. *You're toast. Baked. Grilled. A crispy critter.* We grimace, and look away. Fire wins viciously, gleefully.

Nick whispers swear words under his breath, sweat sliding down his neck from his hairline. We slip and slide quickly down the stairs with the backboard and the body, pushing the spectators aside. We scrape along the hallway and then down the last flight into the street. The ambulance slides away with a wail. Nick is pacing. Alberto fiddles with the oxygen bag. I look up at the sky, where broken clouds stretch over to the horizon, and only look away when Joe calls out that we are leaving.

"Two things," Nick says once we are in the rig. "Two fucking things that scare the shit out of Nick, man." He is paler than usual and shaking. His manic eyes are wider and more bulbous than ever. "Sharks and burns, man," he says, "Those are the ways Nick just doesn't want to die. Sharks and burns."

I don't say anything. What is there to say? Nick puts his head in his hands and says *sharks and burns* to himself again.

By the time we get to the station Nick has stopped wringing his hands. He recounts the story to Alan, but this time he grins.

I think momentarily of calling my friend Eric, a paramedic himself, or calling Melea, or calling my twin, but I decide against it. What would I say? *There was this burned man, see, just melted. And there was nothing I could do, you know? I just let him melt.* Instead, I walk to the kitchen. Hal is the cook today, and a prime example of why firehouse meals have such legendary status. Everything Hal cooks is great-tasting and plentiful.

Even the resident pets gain weight in the firehouse—Station 81 once had a 25-pound cat. None of my cats weigh over 12 pounds; Tom Cat looked like a large blowfish with fur. One day a crew member found a huge rat in the boiler room. The firefighter beckoned Tom Cat over to it but Tom Cat just stared awhile and then ambled away. Like firefighters, Tom Cat liked his meals large, but he was no dummy. Just because the rat lived in the firehouse did not mean it would taste like a firehouse meal.

Tom Cat had acquired the royal tastes of the firefighters he lived with. When he died, he was given a formal burial behind the firehouse. The members dressed in their uniform jackets and ties and saluted while the department chaplain read a few final words. Taps were played, and the flag flown at half mast.

Hal is a big man with a big belly and a voice that precede him. But his paunch is misleading: he is strong and athletic. I have seen him rip a roof apart as he sat on its peak, his legs awkwardly spread. He brought the ax neatly into the steep, thick shingles as if he was halving a sandwich.

"Messy," says Paul, who is helping Hal in the kitchen. He's making patties from hamburger meat and looking down at the oozing meat, he adds, "The guy, I mean."

"Yes, really bad," I say, but my tone is nonchalant.

"What about the Bayshore freeway thing. That was probably worse."

"Those decapitations?" I say, even though I remember right away. It was hard to forget. A large car going 80 miles per hour ran into a sand truck. The car almost came out the other side. Instead, it remained wedged under the belly. Everywhere we moved we stepped on pieces of skull and brain. Later, small images would come to me—the way the top of a scalp sat neatly on the upholstery like a hat, or the sight of the unlucky passenger's long, black hair down the back seat. Just the hair; the head it belonged to was crushed and now the sand truck rested there.

"They were just beside themselves over that accident, weren't they," Paul says, chuckling. "They were in a little over their heads."

"Very funny," I answer. We've nimbly veered away from the burnt man, which is okay by me. The other stories are just as gruesome, but their emotional impact is long gone. It's a strange way to deal with our psyches, a very male way, and today I appreciate it.

The outgrowth of this communication method is the Fire Story, and the Fire Story is a wonderful thing, at once colorful and loud and very funny. I love Fire Stories, though I am not good at telling them.

Instead, I listen. A Fire Story is such that even if you were there, you do not remember the event, because it is transformed, reworked, blown up. There are no lies, per se. Circumstances simply expand or contract like putty. Long lost quotations emerge from places deep in memory. Events from other stories are mysteriously patched in.

But the key to the Fire Story is the speaker, who recreates the event with sprawling and excited words, adds humor liberally, and coats it all with a light overlay of cuss words. The Fire Story rarely gives insight into the deeper emotions of the speaker; it is not expected to. If it did, it would not be a Fire Story. When Nick shapes the burnt man into a Fire Story, he will not mention sharks or burns.

My favorite tale is one that Lieutenant Tom Donald told me a few months back. I began by telling him one of my own: I had just gotten back from a fourth alarm fire on Pine Street. That house was really blazing, *really blowing out the back, really screaming black smoke when we pulled up*.... By the time Rescue 2 arrived, there were already other fire crews inside. The interior of the house was pitch black and we crawled down the hallway towards the heat belly down. There was something bizarre about the house, but in the smoke and excitement it was not until the fire was over that we realized what it was.

The entire apartment was covered in litter.

Not just covered: caked, carpeted, layered in garbage. The garbage was so high that a firefighter, in the dark and confusion, had fallen out of a window. He had fallen 15 feet to concrete below because there was no sill to protect him—the garbage was flush with the bottom of all the frames. Newspapers and beer cans were wedged in a soggy, burnt mat along the hallway. Someone opened a closet and down rained a hodgepodge of cardboard boxes, and it took a few minutes but then we realized they were all take-out food containers, thrown there after the meal until the closet was full. In the back room, where the fire had originated, it took a little time before we saw that among the cat food and ice cream boxes and still more beer cans, lay the body of a man. In death, he and the garbage looked the same, until someone ran a shovel across him accidentally and his rib jutted suddenly through the mess.

Tom Donald is a veteran lieutenant on Truck 64. He listened politely to my own astonishing tale, and then, in true Fire Story fashion, proceeded to amiably one-up me.

"We once had this 350-pound woman," he begins.

"Get out," I say.

"...with one leg."

"No way," I answer.

"And a house full of garbage so deep that we had to crawl the whole way..."

To get into any of the rooms meant squeezing through the upper half of the doorway. The woman, a recluse, had not been seen in awhile, and neighbors were angry about the putrid smell emanating from the house. The fire department was called to do a "well-being check."

"We half-crouched, half-crawled through this place, all garbage. And we couldn't find her anywhere. And we're thinking how in the hell do you lose a 350-pound one-legged woman?"

Small, slanted depressions like runways in the garbage allowed them to slip into this room or that. No luck. After several hours, they were forced to give up. They threw away their fetid uniforms.

"Where was the woman?" I asked, disbelieving, completely drawn into the Fire Story. "Three hundred and fifty pounds and one-legged? Where could she have gone?" Here, Tom smiled triumphantly and delivered his coup de grace.

The woman's body was found two days later. It seems that as the debris took over, the woman decided to dig tunnels through the garbage, thus creating a whole new home. But the garbage had betrayed its owner. A tunnel had collapsed on the woman, suffocating her in her world of Styrofoam and cake tins and newspapers and cat food. Unwittingly, Tom and his crew had been crawling over her decomposing body and an elaborate room and hallway system, itself decomposing too.

I repeat this story to Paul, but I do not have the story-telling skills of a veteran. Paul laughs anyway, wiping his hands on a towel, reaching for a long whip of scallions.

Miller comes back from his medical class mid-afternoon and we decide, with little time left in the day for a dive or a climb, to look instead at the airbags. They are inconspicuous cushions that inflate with an air bottle. The smallest, just five and a half inches square, can lift over three tons. Slid under the offending weight,—a building pillar, a train, an elephant, who knows?—the airbag is filled with air, raising the tonnage from the victim. It seems absurd that this small piece of equipment could literally move mountains. Not so absurd, though, as the loudspeaker that cuts through Joe's lecture and informs us that the hospital needs Rescue 2's assistance in their emergency room.

There is only one reason that an emergency room needs a firefighter more than a doctor.

"I'll bring in the chainsaw," Alberto says in a rare foray into crass humor. The compartment doors are wide open and equipment is being dropped onto the pavement. Air hose, regulator, air bottle. Miller is, as usual, expressionless behind his moustache.

The emergency room doors are held open by a bland-faced security guard, who stares at us, suddenly interested; it is not often that firefighters are summoned to the emergency room, where everything has stopped until they arrive, like highly paid doctors flown in from out of town.

A fire engine crew is already there, shuffling from one foot to the other in succession, half smiles on their faces. When they are dismissed by the chief, they walk away visibly relieved. "Good luck, Squaaaaad," someone says, with a grin. "Yeah, man," someone else sniggers, "Have fun in there."

The chief looks at us. "Keep it professional, okay?" he says. Joe nods and we walk in, greeted by two nurses and our patient, prone on the emergency room table.

The cock ring has been on him for two days, explains a nurse, handing operating room gowns and masks to Miller, Alberto and me. The man is groaning. His hands are spread protectively over his groin, and his eyes are wide with panic. The nurse looks tired and slightly perplexed.

I have never seen a cock ring, though I have heard of them from other Squad members, who have been on calls like this before. The cock ring is a simple device used to maintain erections, and is slid to the base of the penis, behind the scrotum, or in front, depending on your preference, allowing blood to fill the penis for erection, but inhibiting the ebb. Sometimes men wear more than one ring, or they may get creative and use, for instance, a gym weight or a sledge hammer head. The problem is that sometimes the cock ring gets stuck. Then the penis swells far more than it should, becoming purple, then black, heading toward gangrene. In these (true) cases, the emergency room doesn't have the tools to right the situation. That's why the Rescue Squad is called.

"This is going to have to get cut off," the nurse says, pointing.

"We are going to have to cut it off," Alberto repeats cheerfully to the groaning man. "The ring, I mean." The man on the table looks as if he doesn't care about what may have to go, as long as the pain subsides.

Miller begins to hook up our small pneumatic saw, used especially for these cases. There are different bits, but the one for the toughest cases is the circular blade, which we use now. I lean over the man, a boy really, pale and thin with blotchy skin and sandy hair. He looks straight off of a combine in some Kansas wheat field, but I know that instead he is probably a hustler from the Tenderloin. I see that the ring is not made of anything our best blade cannot handle. This is not always the case; once a man used a ring made of a steel so strong that a dentist had to be called in with a diamond bit drill. Since that incident, General Hospital retains a dentist permanently on call in case of other such emergencies.

Miller accelerates the saw for kicks, and it spins with a loud, insistent whine. It looks like he's smiling.

"You take the head and talk to this guy," I say to Alberto. "And I'll pour the water." Water is needed because the ring quickly gets overheated from the friction of the spinning blade.

"I'm not sure I want to take the head," Alberto chuckles.

Miller accelerates the saw again. "This might hurt," Alberto sings.

"I don't care," our patient replies. "Just get the motherfucker off." Then, as if he realizes it is best to keep us on his side, he says, "I'm sorry, I'm not mad at you, I'm just dying here. I'm dying." He pants heavily. "This goddamn hurts."

"Hey, hey, no swearing in here. It will just make things harder, uh, I mean more difficult." Alberto says, smirking.

In fact the penis looks anything but erect. It is swollen and limp, like a thumb recently caught in a door. The cock ring, the young man says, was for his girlfriend, "She wanted it on."

"You're a good man, Charlie Brown," Alberto says, positioning himself with a piece of cardboard.

I hold a cup of water, and a nurse stands near the sink ready to hand me more. A second nurse leans in and forces a tongue depressor under the cock ring, during which time the man screams and pants even more. The tongue depressor is vital. It keeps the swollen skin away from the blade during the cut, and once the cut breaks through the metal, it is the only thing between the blade and his future sex life. Miller pulls his surgical mask and glasses on and revs up the saw again.

"Ready?" the nurse asks.

"Ready," Alberto and I say. Miller just leans in, saw screaming, and begins.

The saw immediately throws a high arc of sparks. Anyone passing by, seeing us in the hospital gowns that cover our thick turnout coats and the masks that cover our face, would have wondered why these doctors were welding in an emergency room. The nurse frantically hands me Dixie cups of water which I pour, then toss aside, reaching for the next. Alberto looks on cheerfully, his job to hold a piece of cardboard at an angle, which wards the hot sparks and splashing water away from Miller. We are an odd emergency team, smelling of old smoke and sterile paper.

Throughout this, the man is screaming, perhaps more from apprehension than anything else, but he remains perfectly still, understanding that any movement could change his life forever. We, for all our joking, do not want a mishap either. A slip would send blood everywhere and, despite our emergency room protection, we know how dangerous that could be.

Every so often, Miller stops the saw to rest and assess the cut. Finally the saw splits the tongue depressor and Miller steps back. He's done a good job, and even I say so. I'm certainly glad that I didn't have to make the cut.

"That wasn't so bad, now, was it?" Alberto says politely. The man reaches for the cock ring to pull it off.

Unfortunately, one cut is not enough to slip the ring off. There will have to be another cut.

"Caroline will do it," Miller says, putting the saw down, not looking at me.

"Ha," I say, thinking that he's simply joking. The idea of a woman with a saw near a penis seems to amuse him.

"Go ahead, Caroline," Miller says again, and now I hear the mockery in his voice.

"No, thanks," I say.

"You'll be fine," Alberto says.

"No, really." I look at Miller. There is defiance in those beady eyes.

Wassamatta? they seem to say. *No guts? Scared? Can't take the heat?* I stare back, equally defiant.

Joe looks up from his clipboard, registers the lull in activity, and frowns. "Let's get this moving," he says, irritated.

He knows what's going on—he's too smart not to—but he's not going to interfere unless it looks like a lawsuit is in the offing. In his view, differences are best fought out by the back fence of the school-yard. Either that or he understands that I'm tough enough to handle this on my own. Whichever one it is he just waves impatiently and the tension becomes thick, so thick I finally give in.

"Okay, okay," I say, as nonchalantly as I can. I take the saw and press the trigger thoughtfully. "You guys are all perverts."

What I'm really worried about is the fact that I have a lazy eye. It doesn't get in the way much, except when I'm tired or under stress. Then it wanders slightly towards my nose. As a result, all my life I have had to overcome problems in depth perception. So far these problems have never amounted to more than a completely whiffed tennis ball, or a wheel against the curb. Today, however, a small problem in depth perception is all that it would take to make a very big problem. I'm sud-denly feeling tired, and definitely under stress.

"Ready, buster?" I lean in as close as possible without seeming pos-itively prurient. I squint. I push the plastic surgical glasses tight against my face. I begin to sweat.

Fuck you, Miller, I say to myself.

The saw hits the ring decisively, and from there I cannot see any-thing but a brilliant array of sparks. "Jesus," I say. I stop the saw, and back away. I expect the penis to be lopped in two, but it remains intact. There is a small new nick in the ring.

"Just getting that starting cut," I say. I laugh nervously. I should stop right here and hand the saw back to Miller, but I can't. To do so would concede defeat. It would admit that I am less able, less agile, less courageous. Of course, the idea that the ability to cut a cock ring off is a measure of success would, in a more lucid moment, be ludicrous. Right now, it seems of utmost importance.

I lean in and squint again, aim and press the trigger once more. At a certain angle, I can just place where the blade is. I fix my eyes on the spot, and try to focus my lazy eye. I could close it, but my right eye is far sighted. The lazy eye, however, is near sighted, so that my vision is the culmination of a curious partnership—two local unions doing separate but closely related jobs.

"Whoa!" yells the nurse.

"Whoa!" yells Alberto.

"Whoa!" yells the man on the table.

I recoil, my arm snapping back, my finger off of the trigger button. I look around casually. "I was on it," I say, picking up the tongue depressor. It is split through. For goodness sake, that was close. "How's the penis?" I ask, as if this were a social nicety.

"Wow," says the young man, panting and holding his traumatized member. "Thank you so fucking much. I thought I was going to die."

"Get one with a latch next time," I suggest.

"I think he likes you," Alberto says, and slaps me on the shoulder, grinning.

17.

The woman is dead. They swear that she has just been talking, that she got up to go to the bathroom and then said something or other to them that no one can remember. "Kicking the H," says another woman. "She was kicking it."

I am the driver today but do not stand outside with the vehicle because on a resuscitation everyone comes in to help. She is still warm and if what the people standing around say is true, she has been down about three minutes. We take her off the bed and lay her on the floor.

Her body is pale and limp. She gazes upward in a blank stare and her mouth falls open to cut a sharp triangle into her face. She is missing teeth, which is no surprise. Teeth don't do well on the streets. They are knocked out by punches, broken by the concrete of the sidewalk, corroded by methamphetamines, or simply loosened and lost by lack of care. I kneel and undo the oxygen bag.

A woman sits in the chair next to a cardboard sign that says Five Dollars to Sleep Here, watching us work. Her hair is dry and thin and forced into unnatural angles by hair spray. Her face is deeply wrinkled, but I guess she's not older than thirty. She's in charge of this apartment, she tells us. She's a longtime heroin addict herself, who gets a little extra money to let people shoot up here. As the sign says, if they want to nod out too, they have to pay more. She doesn't know much about the dead woman except that she's pissed on the sleeping bag, and she's *kicking the H.*

"A little late to kick it," says Joe, stepping around the wet sleeping bag. His scissors ply easily through the thin dirty cloth of her shirt. Alan has the defibrillator machine open and hands Joe the pads. I've put the mask on her face and begun to squeeze it, breathing for her. We're all sweating. Resuscitations are done at a crouch, so we're shuffling like crabs around her, trying to stay out of each other's way. As I watch Joe hover a pad over her chest, I notice something. One breast is bruised. I look closer, wondering whether some blunt trauma to the heart may have killed her. It's then that I see that the skin is pecked with needle marks. Who shoots up in their breast? The left breast too, right over the heart. From the looks of it she also shoots up in her earlobes. Her ankles too. The arm, of course, is long not an option anymore. The skin is brittle and unnaturally white, as if the veins underneath have retreated deep under the dense plain of skin, like hunted animals.

White to right, red to ribs. Joe slaps each pad onto the woman's chest. Sometimes we say it aloud to remind ourselves or just move our lips silently as if in prayer. The machine barks at us in its strange mechanized voice to Stand Clear, and we rock back on our heels, waiting. No shock indicated, the machine says. Joe begins chest compressions.

The paramedics arrive and brandish needles of their own, but as expected the woman's tired veins slip away. Eventually, they decide to use her neck vein, a last resort. We watch and grimace.

Joe stops chest compressions to do paperwork and Alan takes over just as they put epinephrine down the IV and her heartbeat comes back with a bang. We joke that Alan has the doctor's touch and more, that he has a way with the ladies, that he makes their hearts beat faster. We are crude because we have seen all this before, and because there is no family to be worried about. The paramedic grunts and shakes his head and says how most of the hospital people think these medical drugs are just a cruel way to force life back into a body that is already brain dead.

"Put enough epinephrine in," he says, "And a rock will get a heart-beat."

They cart the woman away. Her heart is pounding hard, and Alan is beet red from the teasing. We pack up. "Good job," Joe murmurs, as he always does.

At the station, Joe walks to his desk to fill out the report. There is a crowd around the teletype; the new lieutenant list is being passed around and discussed. Who scored high, who did but shouldn't have, who scored low but will get a job anyway. I don't listen because like others I am tired of the mockery, vitriol, conspiracy theories, and long debates. Maybe it's always been this way, but it seems especially bad these days.

Nick the Paramedic has scored high, and despite the fact that he has only a year and a half on the job, there is no overt anger, just mild joking about how such an unhinged guy could become a lieutenant. This is in sharp contrast to the last lieutenant list. A woman who scored well with less than two years in the department found the words "some-one is going to get killed" next to her name. Understandably she took this to be a direct threat on her life. On that list, four women were appointed officers. All of them tested in the top forty (19th, 27th, 33rd and 39th) out of over 300 test takers. All the women had a tough time. First was the written threat mentioned above. Another woman received threatening phone calls at home, and considered turning down her appointment. Another was openly disobeyed. Another was badmouthed before she even arrived at her station. Nick-with-the-shifting-eyes will get no malicious scribblings, no threatening phone calls, just some rib-bing. Behind his back the men will shake their heads, but partly out of admiration; he must be smart at least, they'll say.

* * *

Interesting things have happened since the 1980s, when the court mandated that San Francisco Fire Department hire and promote along ethnic and gender lines. Some men searched their family trees and have come up (legitimately and otherwise) with roots in protected classes. They have tried to move ahead based on the new classification. Miller, for instance, who complains bitterly about the women, got into the department as an Asian on his mother's side. It is not easy to tell on his physiognomy, and he does not mention it.

Actually, a system of patronage like affirmative action is not new to fire departments. In the late 1800s, a huge wave of Irish and Italian immigrants came to the United States and continued until the first World War. Local mayors, in order to win the immigrant vote, had them hired to local fire and police departments if they promised their support. At the time, the Irish and Italians faced heavy discrimination and disdain, so they knew that this job-for-vote exchange was a good deal for them.

Other people say that police and firefighter jobs are heavily Irish and Italian because city jobs were the only ones that were open to everyone fairly. In the 1930s, the "civil service" department was established to counter high-level corruption. Supposedly, you could no longer pay a high official for a job, nor could he pull strings to get you one; now the civil service sector administered objective tests. This made it possible for people who were discriminated against to get jobs through them. Of course, this did not include blacks or women, so I do not know what to think of this explanation. One way or the other, it remains ironic that almost a hundred years later, these Irish- and Italian-Americans would angrily denounce affirmative action.

It doesn't stop there. For a long time, military veterans automatically got "points" in hiring and seniority in the fire department even if their service had nothing to do with fire. Can it be a surprise that, for many women and people of color, the grumblings of their Caucasian brothers seems hollow and hypocritical?

To make it even more confusing, many firefighters understand that tests, even when they are unaffected by affirmative action, are problematic. If someone does well on one after only two years, as Nick has done, we realize that this does not necessarily make him a good lieutenant. It makes him a good test-taker. Going strictly by the numbers has its problems; experience is imperative. However, the number of years and the kind of experience that makes a good leader are almost impossible to quantify.

Since the advent of the consent decree, San Francisco uses "banding" to rank its tests. This allows latitude to promote people of color and women, as well as a paradigm in which a strict test-taking aptitude is not always rewarded with a job. Banding is a process in which people within a certain range of scores are considered equal, just as a student who gets a 99 on a test and a student who gets a 94 on a test will both be given an "A." Detractors claim that the band range is not related to ability, but is widened or narrowed according to how many minorities are needed to fulfill promotional and hiring goals. Supporters claim that tests are fallible and that a strict numerical ranking only favors the better educated and thus the white test-taker. They also point out that years of not hiring or promoting minorities has in effect "banded" whites for a long time; now it's somebody else's turn. To make matters more controversial, the test results are shrouded in secrecy. None of the test-takers are given an assessment of what they did right or wrong to deserve their score, so that rumors abound of favoritism and false scores. A few years later, a black woman with nine years in the department will score number 3 on the lieutenant test and there will be murmurs that political skullduggery got her there, as if there was no chance that she could have gotten there on her own.

The laughs and snickers around the communications desk increase. Maybe I will go read, hope for a call. As if I have summoned it, the Bee-Bop suddenly sounds.

Rescue 2 to Capp Street. *Well-being check.*

The address is just around the corner. By now, light is fading from the sky. The windows are dark, the thick oak door locked.

We hate well-being checks. We never know what we will find.

"When did you last see him?" Joe asks the neighbor.

The neighbor pauses to think.

"December," he finally says.

"December? December, as in two months ago?"

The neighbor shrugs.

We are not pleased. Joe shimmies up to a window. It opens easily.

"No smell," he says, as he slides into the apartment. That is a good sign. Maybe the guy just up and left. Maybe he retired, moved to Florida. The narrow beam of Joe's flashlight hits the window briefly and then disappears.

Seconds later, Joe speaks.

"I found him," he says, in a calm voice.

The cold weather has kept the man from smelling too much, but the decay is unmistakable. A soft fuzz of mold coats the body, giving it a creepy, hairy look. Blood has congealed underneath it and spread from there like a wrinkled blanket. The fingers and toes have rotted off, leaving clumsy stumps. Most horrific of all is the face, which has fallen in on itself with the weight of time. It looks like a grinning skeleton. It glistens with what I first think is the beam of my flashlight playing funny tricks. I look again. The body is teeming with maggots.

I go back to see the body four times in the twenty minutes it takes for the paramedics to arrive. The first time is duty. The second is to see if I have the stomach to look at it again. But the third and the fourth times are for the pure unadulterated thrill of realizing how alive I am compared to how dead I could be.

Alberto says it is disrespectful to keep staring. Joe just shrugs. It is as if stumbling over a decaying body in the dark is an everyday occurrence for him. In the kitchen, we stop. Incredibly, one burner is on, the blue flame still on its medium setting, a ring of heat glowing heartily.

"Wow," says Joe. He shakes his head, "Now that could have been a good one."

He leans in and switches the burner off. We stare at the greasy, blackened stove and I think of all the ways in which that one flame, in two months time, could have played out each moment. I imagine a fire, where I crawl over the rotting man and the maggots stick to my coat. Instead, by some act of grace, or mercy, it stayed there, looking over its long gone owner like a small halo.

18.

Smell of smoke, shouts. Engine 64 hisses to a stop just a little ahead of the front door. Flames, and a man gesturing wildly. He is barefoot.

I am on the engine today, just for this shift. It is an assignment that I do not mind, especially when there is a fire. Today, I can have the hose. First in, At the Nozzle.

I throw the air pack on, shove my flashlight under a strap, and go for the hose bed. From the corner of my eye I see that the front door is open. Fire runs up the thin stairwell in speckles. Something tells me this is bizarre; the staircase seems to leak flames, long teardrops instead of the robust, full fists of color and heat. As I round the rear of the rig, I see that Don Harris already has a hose line off the engine. I screech to a halt, disappointed. I wanted that nozzle.

But in Harris' hurry to snag the premiere position, he has not yet grabbed his air pack. He is an old-timer, and old-timers have tricks for surviving in the thick poisonous air without a mask; they put their noses right up to the water stream at the nozzle and breathe from invisible air pockets or, in the very early days, they grew long beards, which they pushed to their mouths and breathed through, a crude filter. But those days are gone. Now an air pack is mandated and if you don't use the mask, you're reprimanded. Too many firefighters died early deaths of lung cancer and heart attacks. Even now the average age of death for a firefighter is 58 years old.

I realize that Harris is going for his air pack now. He puts the nozzle on the ground.

First In, I think. At the Nozzle.

I reach in and grab.

If being At the Nozzle is the high point of engine work, losing that position is the most humiliating. To put the nozzle down like that, unprotected, is a cardinal sin. When I have had the nozzle, I have wedged it firmly between my knees. I crouch over it protectively while I quickly jam my air mask on. Now, Harris sees me coming. But for once, being a woman is an advantage. He underestimates me.

The second I pull it from under him he jerks around. *What the goddamn fuck!* he yells. *What the goddamn fuck do you think you are doing?*

Don Harris has almost thirty years in the department. He is Caucasian, with long blonde sideburns and a slow voice. He is a loner, talking to people rarely, never eating a meal with the group, never joining social functions outside the firehouse. He stays up in the dorm by his bed. He watches religious television with the sound turned down on a small black and white television set. He cooks his meals on a portable hot plate. "Don's Diner" they call the corner he partitions off with privacy screens. In this odd igloo, surrounded by rows of beds, he stays all day, a strange, quiet man.

Firefighters are an incurably social group, loud and fun-loving for the most part, and Harris' unsocial attitude can be an affront. So while being a woman may be a disadvantage in the fire department, being a loner is completely unforgivable. But Harris is always decent to me. He says good morning when I greet him and never ignores me more than he ignores anyone else. I like him and, more important, I respect him, because he does exactly what he wants, despite the backlash. And he is a good firefighter.

He yells *Fuck* another time. I drop the nozzle. Partly it is out of shock, partly it is out of respect for his thirty years of experience. Harris grabs it and immediately his anger evaporates; he knows that he would have done the same thing if the situation had been reversed. He heads for the stairs. I grimace at my stupidity; I will not be At The Nozzle now.

Truck 64 pulls in behind the engine. I hear the motor whine as it strains to lift the hydraulic aerial ladder.

Tiny flames are everywhere, like small stars in an evening sky. At the top of the stairs it abruptly becomes midnight, and the short streaks of fire converge into a broader borealis of orange that fades into the smoke. It is hot. I drop as low as I can to the floor while still "pulling line," hauling the heavy hose line so that Harris will not have to stop. He seems to have a sixth sense about where to go; together we twist, turn, thread our way down a hallway.

Afterwards, Harris nods at me. "Good on the line," he says. "I didn't feel it at all." We walk through the charred rooms, picking up a shriveled picture frame, pointing to a melted kettle, marveling at the iron bed-posts, now twisted like candles from the heat. It can be a few hundred degrees on the floor, and it will be over a thousand at the ceiling. A thousand degrees, hovering above me as we crawl. I take off my air pack and wipe my face.

It was not the nozzle, but following an old-timer is the next best thing. I reach under my helmet to push back my hair and the barefoot man pulls at my sleeve.

He is big-eyed. "My wife," he moans. "My wife, I tried to catch her." His hands run up and down his cheeks. "Is she gonna live?"

They had found the wife. She lay crumpled below her third-floor window, and the ambulance had whisked her away. I put my hand on his shoulder. *I tried to catch her,* he says again and spreads his arms wide to show me. He seems to be in shock, slow-moving, repeating himself. My heart contracts and I murmur something semi-intelligible. *I'm sorry, sir. Sorry.*

A burly man in a blue helmet taps a clipboard and then his cheek with a pencil. Fire investigators ask the first crew what they saw in order to determine the origin of the fire. I describe the way the door was wide open, the way the fire freckled the staircase.

"Yuh," the fire investigator says, nodding. "Molotov cocktail alright."

Awfully fishy, he explains, that the front door was open. He tilts his chin towards the husband: seems the husband woke up and left his wife sleeping to get some sugared donuts. "Sugared donuts," he repeats, shaking his head. "At two in the morning."

"The husband says that when he returned with the donuts the house was on fire. The door," adds the fire inspector, "was already wide open, with no damage to the lock, nothing."

Jump, jump, the husband had urged the wife from the ground. Jump.

The police lead the husband away. I take off my gloves absently, then put them on again. I am anxious because I have given something to the husband. I have doled out precious emotion, and it was wasted. In the emergency services business, feelings are finite. We guard them as if they might leak away completely if we permit any small opening.

I pick up an axe. Usually the chiefs put Rescue 2 back into service quickly, leaving other crews to pick up the mess. But today I'm on the engine, so overhaul is included. I like overhaul. I understand better what Captain Leahy told me so many years ago. *Look at the way it is put together.* Today there is a lot to pull apart; the walls are wrinkled black and look like they will crumble with a slight push. But that is not true; swinging an axe is hard, dirty business. If you're not in shape it will tire you out within a few swings, and even if you are, you learn not to fight the wood but to nurse it apart, peering carefully at its grooves and its hinges.

The lathe and plaster give way easily, in snaps and pops like breaking ribs. Tile splits neatly if the edge goes in right. The burned material goes in a pile that will be pulled out later, dumped in the street, and sprayed down.

The bathroom wall is burned underneath. I call Ralph over to show him. Ralph used to play with the 49ers. Not with the 49ers, he corrects, *for* the 49ers. He was hired to play in training against the team, but he was never part of it.

"Okay, babe, we'll pull the wall down from the other side too." Ralph calls everyone "babe." He's big and bearish and no one seems to mind.

Ralph yells to no one in particular that the closet behind the bathroom needs to be taken apart. Someone asks for an axe.

"Give him your axe, babe, will you?"

Yeah. Right. I step over the wreckage. No one gives up their equipment. I'm certainly not going to.

I walk toward the closet. "I'll do it," I say cheerfully, and try to step in.

Miller blocks the opening. He reaches for the axe.

"I'm already here," he says, without looking at me directly.

"I'll do it," I repeat.

"Give me the fucking axe," he says, his voice low and menacing. He draws out each word, as if they are evenly weighted and all mean *fucking.*

"Get your own axe, I'll do it." I move forward, shielding the axe with my body. Ralph is behind me and says nothing. Miller does not move.

This is a standoff where the struggle between being a team player and an individual comes to a head. It is hardly worth grousing over an axe if the wall should come down. But it is my axe; I went and got it for myself. And it is Miller who is challenging me, who hates me, and everything he thinks I stand for. Ironically, what he thinks I stand for is weakness, cowardice and an unwillingness to do the hard work, clearly not true, since I'm the one demanding that he step aside.

By now, he looks uncomfortable. It is clear that he did not bring in anything, and he oversteps the code by insisting that I give him an axe after I have refused, once, twice, three times. No one else says anything.

Miller does not step aside. Do I push by him? Do I turn away so no one can bring down the wall? Do I stand here forever? Ralph still says nothing.

I hand him the axe.

"Get your own axe next time, Miller," I hiss.

"Eat shit, bitch," he says, and turns away.

19.

The water is cold. From where I float in it, I can see two detectives standing on the dock, staring at the ground. They point to where the gun was found, and to the blood drops. They make a wide sweep with their hands. They adjust their ties, narrow their eyes, nod thoughtfully. Police gestures, for a police action.

The wetsuit is warmer now, and the detectives look at the water and say a word to my tender. My tender is Lt. Green, and he is a highly excitable man, excited at the prospect of a body recovery, excited that his diving lessons are at work. He always wants to go into the water himself; he has been known to strip off his uniform and dive after a car in a lake in only his underwear, despite his own warnings that all of us are to follow all safety rules strictly. I like Sean Green; his passion is infectious. When he's really excited, he leans in close and yells, spit flying.

The body will probably not be here; the tides pull everything out quickly and efficiently. The suicide note found on the man's bed was written two days before, and it directed the detectives to the gun and the blood and the narrow, empty dock. Still, I wonder if they suspect foul play. It is hard to shoot yourself and then fall into the water, leaving the gun neatly behind.

I suited up on the way to the incident, my back turned from Tim, who was suiting up as well. To put on a wetsuit in a wildly careening vehicle is a miracle of agility. There is a story about two Rescue 2 members who were likewise threading their feet into the tight neoprene when the rig slowed abruptly and they were thrown to the ground. They lay momentarily hog-tied in each other and their suits, and when they looked up they caught sight of the woman in the car behind, aghast at these half-naked men entwined and struggling.

Today is not my regular shift, so I feel lucky that I am working anyway and can do this body recovery. Still, a part of me loathes the prospect of what I could find. Diving is an exciting experience, but rescue dives are marred by the fact that the San Francisco bay becomes pitch black a few feet below the surface. The only way to search is by touch. This means hands outstretched and sweeping back and forth, through the few feet of pure, thick silt. You touch other things—bottles, cans, twisted metal slick with algae—but anything could be an arm, or a grinning macabre face. A drowned body is not a pretty thing. Bloated, often eaten away by crabs, it is the Monster Under the Bed, The Noise in the Closet, anything you dreaded as a kid. But now there's no time to be freaked out. Green is waving his arms, signaling that it's time for the search to begin, so I hold the rope in the correct hand and let myself sink below the surface.

I'm descending, slowly. The light fades to brown and then suddenly, as if someone turned out the lights, to black. Moments later, I reach the silt. I exhale deeply to penetrate, and descend through the ooze, finally finding the hard, flat bay floor. I sit here for a moment. It's a common mistake for a rescue diver to be too high, unwittingly running hands over the top of the mud, missing the bottom entirely. Slowly I turn and lie prone, then wait another moment to make sure I have the right buoyancy. In no time, I feel scratching on my arms, my legs, up my back. Even through the thick wetsuit, it's there. No need to panic, I know what this is. It's the crabs, scurrying all over me. They'll accompany me for the whole search.

I remind myself where I am—the bottom of the bay—and that in my left hand is the rope, a communication tool and a lifeline, that leads to the surface. All is well, I tell myself. I take a few breaths, then I tug once, feel the responding tug back, and begin to swim.

There's a tendency to want to bolt away, to shake the crabs loose, for one, and to get on with the search. But too much fin movement can raise you too high off the bottom. And you have to go slow to make sure you don't miss anything. Besides, swimming too fast looks panicky, and while they cannot see my face, they can see my bubbles, which become the measurement of coolness and skill.

So I move my legs just enough, and sweep my hands back and forth in wide arcs, as if erasing a blackboard, trying to feel for the body. Instantly I come across all sorts of debris—hard objects, twisted objects, soft objects, sharp objects, all the detritus of the world above, thrown from boats, washed from gutter pipes. I can't see what I'm touching, but I guess what they are anyway: a shopping cart here, pipes, cans, bottles there. No body yet. And always the crabs, running across my back like a million tiny fingers.

Green tells us that we have to picture what we are looking for, picture it well, in order to keep from confusing it with all the other bottom-dwelling debris. But I know all about bodies that have been in the water too long, with their eaten-away faces (the eyes a special delicacy), and bloated bodies that pop when touched, releasing a noxious smell and the sea animals dining there. I don't want to think of all that so instead I decide to imagine a red and white plaid shirt. No one told me what the missing man was wearing, but for now, in order to keep the heebie-jeebies in check, it will have to do.

Two tugs from the surface tell me to turn around. This is a major feat in heavy darkness, a different matter entirely from turning around in daylight. There's no reference point here, nothing to judge where I am, so the trick is to keep track of my body in reference to itself.

This means careful movements, done in slow succession: first, the rope switched to my other hand, then the arm extended ninety degrees from the body. Ninety degrees from my body in total darkness is a peculiar thing. It is a feeling from the clavicle of a special tightness, and then a consciousness of the elbow being a certain distance away, of the knuckles at a particular tautness and the wrist extended. Having gained all this, I swim away from that hand, but keep it in place. The rope, which has been let out by Green a few feet, suddenly goes taut, and my search continues.

I haven't been down long, but I've quickly acclimated. The roar of my own breath as it slides past my ears seems natural. The thick silt is soft on my cheek. The bottom takes form, its strange, tangled skin brownish green. I reach and pull at warts and bumps, bringing up old cans and bottles slick with algae. A fish here, there, and always the fine, misty mud. My arm sweeps as if unfurling a cape, and I see that my fingers are spread wide so as not to miss that red and white plaid shirt…

…but it's bullshit, of course, just my mind playing tricks. I can't see a thing. It's still pitch black down here, as I realize when two tugs from the surface signal me to turn around again. More time passes, and then Green pulls on the line three times, indicating that I am to surface.

"It's gone," he yells, leaning down from the dock. "The sea has got him, no doubt about it." Spit flies. He puts up four fingers, indicating that this call is over. "We're going home." He grips my shoulder enthusiastically, then motions for us to head back to the station.

By Friday, I am back in Spokane, Washington, where I have been once every month for the past three months. No scuba diving here; the rivers are frozen and as I doggedly pick up the megaphone and plant myself at the corner, it begins to snow. Behind me is the Spokane Federal Courthouse. Like many evangelists, I fix my gaze twenty or so feet in front of me, so that I can ignore any insults but engage with any willing onlookers. Alexandra has picked the middle of the sidewalk, and since we only have one megaphone between us, she passes out pamphlets. By this time, the citizens of Spokane know who we are. Some wave or nod congenially as they hurry by. Some stop and talk. We look harmless, if earnest. The newspapers have portrayed us as interesting specimens, at the very least. Besides, one of us is on TV.

"You're the ones whose brother is in jail," an elderly man says, the sides of his plaid cap swaying in the wind like an extra pair of ears. I nod. "Well, he's doing the right thing. Not that we are agreed on this animal rights stuff. But he's doing the right thing, not saying anything." The man shuffles away, tugging at his cap. Alexandra and I look at each other. We go back to our positions on the sidewalk.

Jonathan is in jail here, though not considered a criminal, locked up but not under arrest. For the past three months my family and smatterings of his friends have come here to protest his incarceration. Spokane knows us. The taxi drivers yawn and ask, "How's your brother?" when we hail them from the airport upon arrival. "Tell him us taxi guys are behind him. Not on the political stuff. But this grand jury thing. It's the government gone crazy."

The fire department knows nothing about my monthly evangelism. I don't tell them because I am sure that they will not understand. I myself hardly understand. The grand jury is an arm of the government I have only read about briefly in connection with Oliver North. Until my brother is subpoenaed to appear in front of one, grand jury is just a vague legal term.

The grand jury wants to know about my brother's animal rights friends. Jonathan refuses to talk and is thrown in jail. This is, we are told, not a punishment. He is guilty of nothing, they say, charged with no crime. He is not even considered a suspect in the case the grand jury is investigating. Jail time is to "persuade" him to speak.

How can I explain this to the fire department? They will write it off as another liberal scuffle and eccentric tic of the Paul family. I will once again be "different." Even my outside acquaintances, good liberals, good college educated liberals, stare at me blankly and say, well, shoot, he should just talk if he hasn't done anything.

I have my litany down cold. "This is a democracy?" I say to passing cars. "Where someone who has done nothing can be thrown in jail?" Pale faces peer at me from behind the blink of windshield wipers. "Not allowed a lawyer—forced to answer every question." The light changes and the cars slide away. "Is this Turkey, or Russia, or Burma?" The street is empty now but I continue anyway. I have felt much better, much safer in the hottest fires. There, I have my colleagues, whom I trust and admire. Here, the snow begins to fall with a vengeance.

20.

The full box at the projects quickly becomes a second alarm, but by the time Rescue 2 arrives, the fire is out. The chief on duty tells us to wait right here next to him, and he points sternly, knowing that we might try to sneak in anyway, then he ducks his head to speak into his radio. When he turns back to us his face is pale and drawn.

"We're missing some civilians," he says. "I'm pulling everyone out. Body recovery. You're going in."

"What're we looking for?" Joe says.

The chief squares his shoulders.

"One adult, five children."

We decide to work the two bedrooms first. An arson investigator follows with a notepad in his hand, and tells us bits and pieces—the boyfriend smoking and drinking, falling asleep, awaking with the couch on fire, yelling to the residents upstairs: his girlfriend, their 8 year old daughter, and his girlfriend's three grandchildren, the youngest of whom is 8 months old. Then he flees.

"Bastard," the arson investigator says under his breath.

Alberto and I get on our hands and knees and begin. We push, pull, pick with our fingers. The charred debris is matted together by heat and water and the weight of heavy boots, but we try not to use our crash axes. We don't want to puncture a body; we don't want to disturb it at all. It looks crazy really: us moving slowly and precisely, in the posture of people looking for a contact lens, while around us is the mayhem of destroyed walls and ceilings, dripping water, blackened furniture, charred clothes, disintegrating rugs. We're not even sure what the bodies are going to look like, except that the organs, which burst from heated skin, are usually the easiest to see.

It doesn't take long. "Found one," I say, as a reddish, white appears from under the black crust I've been swimming my hands through. Both Alberto and I take a deep breath, then rock back on our heels to collect ourselves. Burned people are tight skinned, no-skinned, burst skinned, shiny red, shiny black, shiny white. It always takes a moment to process. The body goes from looking like debris, to looking abruptly unlike debris, to taking the shape of a human hand, face, or leg.

"We got one," Joe says soon after, from the other room.

"Four more," the arson investigator murmurs.

Alberto and I keep going, picking and pulling and pushing, until ribs stick out. An adult, sideways on the ground. More digging. "Whoa," says Alberto under his breath.

The remains of an infant are tucked under one of the dead woman's arms. Under the other arm, the remains of a child. The woman seems to be curled over, trying to shield them, and then when that is fruitless, trying to comfort. I imagine the scene, the woman grabbing the children to bring them to safety, and then whispering something in the last seconds. The panic, the fear, the love—it's all there, seared into place. There is something so heroic about her posture, and so futile.

Joe walks over. The other three have been found the same way, all together, clutching each other. "Goddamnit," he says, shaking his head. Alberto and I get up slowly. The chief makes a point to tell each of us personally that we've done a good job.

* * *

We are offered stress counseling, but we all refuse it, to my knowledge. It's not that I don't think stress counseling has its place—I do. I simply have no idea what I would want to say about this incident. It seems I am the lucky one, the one who didn't die, so what is there really to talk about? I don't want to be dramatic, or dwell on it, or make it into something that it's not. And yet I want to feel it, or else I've missed an opportunity to fully experience what is happening. It's always a tough balance. How do I stay attached to what is going on emotionally, and yet still maintain enough of a wall to take the action that is required? How much compassion can I access without breaking down? How steeled can I be without losing my humanity? It's the biggest struggle a firefighter faces, I think. Personally I have yet to get it right. I once did CPR on an infant, on the street and in the ambulance all the way to the ER and just as we were turning to leave, a doctor came out and told us before they told the mother: the baby is dead. We stared at him. Dead? We already knew it, it was clear back in the ambulance. But until it's pronounced it's not yet quite true, especially when it's a baby. Then it went like this: Turn around in the hallway of the ER, don't look back, don't look at each other, and don't look in the waiting room when you walk by. Don't talk. Don't even think too much about it.

I do have a coping mechanism. It's a strange method, a little humiliating, probably not the healthiest way to handle things, but here it is: I cry while driving. Always alone, always in my car, always suddenly. When it first happened, I was perplexed and blamed it on the news story I was listening to, and the next time, the song. But deep down I knew it was neither of these. So now I drive and cry and drive, and then I feel better. Sometimes I pull over, but mostly I don't.

I pick up my gloves from the furnace room. I've hosed them down, and now they're dry and clean, so I shove them into my pocket. When a full box comes in later that day, I pull them on. Seconds later, I'm puzzled. I can smell perfume, but it's not coming from me, and surely it's not coming from Alberto.

It's coming from the gloves.

We return home and I shake the gloves off, and march to the hose, and once they're thoroughly soaked I hang them again, and use my spare pair. The honest truth is that I would have preferred blood and guts lodged in the seams, which would only have been disgusting. The woman's perfume is another matter. It's almost like a ghost, hovering nearby. The next shift I pick the gloves up again, and this time bring them to my nose and smell them tentatively. She's still there. I stand for a moment, then I lay the gloves carefully into a waste basket.

A week after the body recoveries, off-duty, I drive down a side street near my home, and quietly begin to weep.

"This department is like a broken marriage," Amy tells me, shaking her head. Amy has a degree in clinical psychology, which she constantly applies to her job as a firefighter. Before she was a firefighter, Amy was a trucker. "And like a broken marriage," she says in her Long Island accent, "there are too many lawyers." When she says "lawyers", she sighs to punctuate her unhappiness. Amy is rarely unhappy, but discontent in the firehouse upsets her because she is on friendly terms with everyone, black, white, male or female. Everyone loves Amy.

She came in around the same time I did and though on the surface our careers parallel each other, in many ways they do not. "I want your defenses," Amy says to me often. "Maybe it is because you don't get along with your mother,"—"muddah" is the way she says it—"but you have good protective mechanisms. Me, I'm an open book. I've got to learn to be more like you, you know?"

Amy is an open book, which accounts for her popularity with everyone in the department. The most grizzled veteran firefighter will break into a grin when Amy enters the room. Even Miller smiles and blushes when she greets him. Perhaps even Todd Lane, the man who tried to ostracize me through his all-meat meal, would melt in her presence. Amy has the uncanny ability to make anyone feel comfortable, with a combination of humor, openness, and a genuine lack of cynicism. Amy simply goes on being Amy, no matter whom she interacts with. I envy Amy's openness, we all do.

"Yeah, well, Caroline, you are always in control," Amy says. "It's your muddah, I am sure. She hurt that little girl in you."

After breaking up with her girlfriend of three years, she shed some tears in the firehouse, whereupon the guys tried to comfort her with typical firehouse advice.

"Firefighters don't cry," they said. "Especially not over a woman."

"Hey, guys," she answered, "I'm having a moment. Okay? I'm having a moment."

She would gesture with her hands and unabashedly tell them that they repressed their feelings too much. They would shake their heads and smile indulgently and say mournfully that this was what the new fire department was coming to.

When I hand over the air pack to Patty Schecter I think she may fall down; she is already breathing heavily under the combined weight of my turnout coat, turnout pants, and a helmet that sags dangerously on her head.

"About thirty pounds," I say, nodding at a Rescue Squad air pack. She grimaces. She is, after all, not a firefighter. She is a lawyer. But I do not want her to back out of this before I have made my point. Quickly, I hand her the axe, which she takes with reverence. She shuffles over to look in the mirror, eyes shining despite the exertion. "Wow," she says quietly. Lost in a daydream of her own, she forgets I'm even there. I walk a few steps away, to let her live this out. I know how it's going to go—everyone does it and sure enough she does it too; when she thinks I'm not looking she lifts the axe for a surreptitious pose. *I'm a firefighter!*

Patty Schecter is actually the federal court monitor, a lawyer assigned to oversee the implementation of the consent decree in the San Francisco Fire Department. She has a soft, even voice that belies her authority. Her neat red hairstyle and pale, freckled skin give her a pleasant, unassuming look, though her precise dictum indicates that she is not someone to be taken lightly. She has listened carefully to what I have to say, nodding at times, or taking notes. She has gamely put on my equipment; now she shuffles back to me ready to take it off.

"It *is* heavy," she agrees.

"And you've only had it on for a minute or so. Imagine being soaking wet, carrying hose—another sixty pounds—up a stairwell. Or swinging that axe—seven pounds—to get through a roof."

There have been many lawyers involved in the fire department and its troubles since I entered the job. Things have improved under their watchful eye, things that have helped everyone, male or female. There are separate bathrooms, better protective clothing, more specific management directives, an environment that strongly forbids certain harassments. But a major problem remains. I have come to clarify to her the physical demands of the job and I want to make the lawyers understand how important it is that not just women should be admitted to the department, but that *strong* women should be.

The lawyers are, after all, lawyers. They do not do heavy manual labor. They have no idea of the strength required for firefighting.

"Why don't you put the mask on?" I open up the tank on Patty's back. She is sweating now, visibly uncomfortable. The air hisses, and I show her how to press the mask to her face, then pull the straps tight. "Breathe," I command, and she does, her eyes widening, the regulator honking. She pulls the mask off quickly. It's claustrophobic to anyone not used to it. But that's okay, I'm sure my point has been made: this job is tough, made for a certain type of person and definitely a certain type of woman.

"What about the men? Aren't there weak men?" Patty says.

"Of course. This is not exclusively a gender thing."

"Or an affirmative action thing," Patty adds.

"Look, at this point you lawyers have everyone so scared of lawsuits that no woman can get fired without everyone jumping to the conclusion it is somehow sexist." I ease the air pack off of Schecter's back and lay the axe on her clean rug. I help her shrug off the final layer of protective clothing. She glances at her watch and tells me she needs to pick up her daughter soon.

"Look," I continue quickly, "Everyone has the same goal. Get qualified people in. And qualified does inherently mean diverse. You and the Union are not as far apart as either of you think."

She looks unconvinced. It seems to be this way with the rest of the lawyers associated with the consent decree.

Patty Schecter is a recently appointed monitor, whose job it is to oversee department changes, but she is not the first of the lawyers I have approached. Before her came a brief but frustrating experience with someone named Jennifer Karl.

I foresee no problems when I enter her office. I assume, wrongly it turns out, that she and I would have a lot in common. Our liberal outlooks would easily mesh; our feminist agenda would coincide; our mutual over-education would ensure downright chumminess. Like Karl, I am a firm proponent of affirmative action, despite the fact that it is not a perfect system. And so I sit down thinking that our conversation will go well. Jennifer Karl will listen closely, even with interest, to my concern that the physical entrance exam is way too easy, and in its current form does women a great disservice.

The change I propose is not radical. I explain my position carefully: I want women in. But this job is a physical one, and higher physical standards are vital to ensure that the strongest women possible get into this changing San Francisco fire department. Change the entrance test, I ask, make it better, harder, more applicable. Do that and we'll get the best women into the SFFD.

Jennifer Karl waits until I am done, then she looks at me with hard eyes and an expression of disdain.

"The standards of that test have been approved by experts," she says slowly. "Statistically, its pass/fail rate is such that it does not bias women or minorities."

"I don't know about statistics," I say. "I just know the real world. The test is too easy."

She pauses, seems to grimace, then speaks even more slowly, as if our disagreement is simply a matter of my lesser intelligence.

"A harder test would have an adverse impact on women," she says.

"Adverse impact" is a legal term to describe a situation in which there is a "significant disparity" in the test scores of different classes. The exact disparity varies according to the case, but the Uniform Guidelines on Employee Selection Procedures, a federal regulation, suggests that if one class' pass rate is less than 80% of the pass rate of the top scoring class, this strongly points to an unfair test. These are the guidelines that the San Francisco Fire Department are held to, and Jennifer Karl is suggesting that women would fail miserably if the test became harder.

If the test does have an adverse impact, this alone will not nullify the results. The test, however, must go on to prove that it is job-related. This was where the San Francisco Fire Department fell short during the 1970s and 1980s. It could not show that their physical or written tests were valid. The third time that the courts asked them to show them job-related test procedures, the city agreed that the tests were no good.

The current test was not put in place, as many people think, in order to lower standards for women and minorities. It was an attempt to improve upon previous, poorly designed tests. I am not a test expert, but I am a firefighter. The current physical test in the San Francisco Fire Department does not seem to me to be job-related either. It is only a compromise between two tired, angry and frightened factions.

148   Caroline Paul

"Besides, the current standards were set by firefighters in the department," she says, a little smug. I know this; the standards were set by the test scores of the lowest performing firefighters in the department. The legal reason behind this was that a firefighter already in was assumed to be qualified for the job. Therefore the lowest test scores reflected the minimum standard necessary to perform firefighting tasks.

"But those standards suck!" I am angry now, and dismayed at our growing antagonism. "The fattest guy in the department is not a good measuring stick for a good firefighter. Look, for all your statistics and your legal minimum standard this and that, all I can say is that this is a test that can be learned in such a way that it does not measure strength at all, it just measures an ability to learn a skill and perform it in a required time. This is going to backfire on all of us."

I sputter out; Jennifer Karl looks at me and then at her watch. (Lawyers do a lot of watch-looking, I have found.)

"Look," I say, trying calm down. "I don't understand why you are against a tougher standard. At least this test should be taken with the gear that we wear—helmet, coat and air pack. That would make it very "job related", which has always been the major concern."

Jennifer Karl reaches for papers, but I do not take the hint.

"I came here on my own," I say. "I'm not doing this for anyone but myself." She lifts the stack of memos and does not answer. "Look, can't we understand each other? We're on the same side … " I'm almost pleading now, a little pathetic, but unable to stop. "I can't figure out why you're so against this," I finally whine, defeated.

She glares at me.

"There is a history of institutional racism and sexism…"

"Please, I know all that. But part of this is about people, not these vague institutions you talk about. You don't really know what day to day life in the firehouse is like. I appreciate all you've done, really, but there has to be room for the gray areas. There just has to be."

But there can't be, not for the lawyers and Jennifer Karl, who stands up to shake my hand stiffly. I do not try to talk to the lawyers again until I meet Patty Schecter and she obliges me by putting on full gear, which is the only means I can think of to drive my point home. It doesn't matter in the end, because the test doesn't change, and I resign to the fact that it probably never will.

The man stands on the second floor fire escape as we pull up, waving his arms and screaming "Fire!" and then he jumps. He writhes on his back and the crowd that has gathered surges forward as if a bag of money has been dropped. A collective breath escapes in a long *whoosh*.

I turn on my air pack with one hand, grip my axe with the other. We can smell the smoke. People are streaming down the stairs. I beat Miller to the door—a private dig that I know he understands—and up the stairs. I push past people who hold hands to their faces and cough. On the second floor the engine crew turns left, dragging the hose down the hallway. They've made a decision, and it's just a guess, for now. There's no visible fire yet. This is a tense time. These hotels, old and rundown and unkempt, wind around themselves like an Escher painting—the same brown doors and yellow walls forever.

I knock impatiently on these brown doors, then push them open and tell the occupant to leave, *now*. If locked, I turn my back and kick them in, using the mule kick. The doors here are weak, the locks cheap, and they break open on the first try.

Miller and I usually avoid being partners; when the Squad splits up into two teams I usually go with Joe. But today Joe is not the officer. Today's officer is Lt. Walden, who has insisted that the least experienced firefighter go with him. This is silly, as it quickly becomes clear that Walden isn't really sure what a Squaddie is supposed to do, making him the least experienced of all. But he's the boss, so no one says anything, and since John Fisher is the "detailed" member today, he goes with Walden, leaving Miller and I reluctant partners.

I tell Miller that I'm going upstairs to search the next floor. He doesn't say that he'll go with me, which doesn't surprise me, but he grins suddenly, which does.

"Okay," he says. "I will be right here when you get back." When I get to the top of the next stairwell I understand his sudden congeniality. The stairwell leads to the roof. I laugh in spite of myself—I should have realized from the outside how many stories high the hotel is. An old-timer will waggle his finger and tell you: notice the exits! Notice the layout of the floor you are on! Where are the windows? Where do the stairwells meet? Do you have at least two paths of egress? It is important to see these things before you enter. One point for Miller.

I bound back down the stairs; the hallway has gotten darker and suddenly down to the right I see that telltale glow, as if the sun is setting gloriously through a window. The engine crew and their hose have gone the other way, so we need our own water up here, fast.

I shout down the stairwell, and someone yells back that a line is on the way. Both Miller and I are poised at the end of the banister, masks on, ready to intercept the nozzle—take it from whoever is coming up. The smoke gathers quickly now; a figure suddenly emerges from below.

It's our Rescue Squad guest, John. He has the nozzle cradled in his arm like a football. One shoulder is dropped to ward us off—he knows his teammates well. He stares straight ahead and—because he has not yet taken the time to put his mask on—I can see that his jaw is set in an unusually determined line. Both Miller and I stop our sudden lunges— John, sweet, polite, choirboy John—looks like he might bite our necks if we so much as reach for the hose. Simultaneously, both Miller and I decide not to fight for it—he has earned it. It's the only thing that Miller and I have ever agreed on.

Lt. Walden is at my shoulder. He yells something at me. Miller has gone down the stairs to pull line. I push John forward, but simultaneously Walden has his hand on my shoulder pulling back. He shouts to slow down, be careful, go easy. Who is this guy? We have no time for such caution.

Just as we reach the corner of the hall, and feel the fire off to the left, we run out of hose. We strain against it, hoping that it is momentarily caught, but it isn't, we've just come up short. So we hunker down. The black settles on us like a wide hot sea, the heat on us, lazy kelp. John swings the water in a wide loop to cool us down. The water falls back searingly hot; it sneaks into my collar and down my back. When orange flashes above us, fleeting shadows of color, I point upward even though I know John can't see my hand. I'm thinking about how fast the fire can race over us and come down behind, trapping us in this ugly dark corridor, so that we are efficiently cremated among the macaroni and cheese cartons, porn films and old newspapers. Quickly I go no further with this thought, knowing that this is tricky territory, where the mind becomes dangerous. In a fire you have to switch some parts off. In my case, I tend to switch too much off, and barrel ahead without thinking—it's a fault of mine that means I would never make a good officer. Walden on the other hand, hasn't switched enough off. He's thinking rationally when he fears the ceiling may fall in, the heater tank nearby explode, the fire leap around suddenly to embrace us with a wide, toothy grin. But it's too rational. After all, the most rational conclusion is that one shouldn't run into a fire in the first place. So it's a balance between understanding the dangers when it's necessary, but not dwelling on them when it's not. I wish I had that balance. The best firefighters do.

I swing my flashlight into the window next to me and then break from my crouch to lean through the frame to break another nearby. Lt. Walden grabs my coat again, yelling something through his air mask. He does not want me to lean out the window in case something falls from above. I think, in light of where we are at this moment, deep in the bowels of a burning residential hotel, that his concern is misplaced.

With the window open, the hallway starts to clear a little. John remains in his linebacker crouch; the fire is in no mood to back down. We're deadlocked at this corner, neither of us able to advance. It feels as if we may stay here forever, locked in a showdown. But we know that the fire has the advantage. It's gathering energy, consuming fuel, getting hotter and angrier by the second. We are wearing down: soon our air packs will signal that our air is running out, or the heat will get so intense that our helmets will blister, along with our ears. The crew behind us may take over or all of us may have to back out.

We hear yelling in front of us—a crew has come around the back of the hotel and taken the fire from the rear. Part of us is mad—*this one is ours, and hey, you could've pushed the fire on us.* But we're fine, with just egos wounded, so the other crew pays no attention. Richard laughingly puts his arm around me when the smoke clears. "Whatsammatta, squaaaaddddeee," he says, elongating the words so they hang in the air as long as possible. "Had to call us to handle this one, dinnchya, huh? huh? dinnchya!"

Later we find out that this fire was arson. A prostitute, angry when the landlord tells her she can't entertain johns here, returns a few hours later with one of those johns, and together they pour gasoline on her bed and drop a match. It seems incredible that they are willing to torch the entire building and everyone in it, but when people are enraged, they often turn to fire to express themselves. In doing so, they're following in the footsteps of the divine. The Christian God of the Old Testament and the Greek gods on Olympus all used fire to wreak revenge. When the Hawaiian goddess Pele is jealous, she leaks lava from her pores; the volcano Kilauea erupts. Fire and high emotion are inextricably entwined. Arson is the ultimate crime of passion.

Revenge fires are actually only one kind of arson fire. Kids who play with matches are responsible for about half of the deliberately set fires in the United States.

Fires set for profit are also a common type of arson fire. Unlike the other two, this type is carefully planned. These fires are usually started in the back, so that they are spotted late, and near the top floor so that the roof burns through. When that happens, the building is exposed to the elements, which ensures a higher payment from the insurance company. Also, if the fire is near the top of the building, water from the fire hoses runs through to the floors below, causing even more damage. Back in the 1970s and early '80s, a lot of San Francisco's real estate was torched for the insurance money. Veteran firefighters talk of whole neighborhoods on fire, night after night. "Back when the Fillmore was burning," they say, as if the fires were not just fires, but calendars by which other events were tracked: *back when the Haight was on fire* or *while the church over on Geary was still standing...* And I listen, imagining whole blocks aflame.

Overall, fire calls are down these days. New building codes, fewer careless smokers, more smoke detectors, higher property values, better fire prevention inspections all have helped. But arson is a fire fueled by some of our most primal emotions; it will not easily disappear.

Now we climb back into the rig slowly. I am tired and my turnout coat, matted against me by water and sweat, feels punishingly heavy. "Man," John says excitedly, as the rig pulls away from the curb. "Man oh man. That was great." I laugh in agreement. The sour stench of burnt wood clings to me. "You guys wanted that nozzle, didn't you," he continues. "You were about to slug me, I swear. And we hit the end of the hose and the corner was right there, right there, and we couldn't go any further and it was hot! Geez, it was hot."

John rarely talks like this. But I understand his sudden outburst. Our everyday selves have scattered suddenly, replaced by something wilder. This is what fire does and, frankly, we just can't help it.

21.

The parking lot behind Walgreens is quiet, and I'm surprised. Even though it is midnight, this is the Mission District on a Saturday night. Quiet moments are rare here. We pull into the large, gray shadows, our emergency beams dropping red swatches of light across the buildings. We see a few cars, an open dumpster, a stray newspaper. Otherwise, nothing.

I look up at the sky. It's a full moon. Firefighters understand the power of a full moon—it makes people crazy. We will gaze at the sky all evening and nod: An arson fire is likely, or a few shootings. Tonight, at least, we will feel that there is some reason for the cruelty, the chaos. We can point to the large squat moon and say, there, that's why.

Someone steps into the headlights, a young man, pale and small-faced, with the faint stitching of moustache on his upper lip. He beckons us with the urgent wave, then runs off to the left. We swing around, following him. A small woman with long dark hair steps from the shadows. The man puts his arm around her.

"I'm pregnant," the woman whispers as we approach.

"You're pregnant?" I say, though I heard her. "How pregnant?"

"Very pregnant," the young man interrupts. "Like, she's contracting and stuff."

I see now: her stomach, and the stain down her jeans that indicates her water has broken. Her labor pains are two minutes apart. The next one hits her and she sags into the young man's arms. I look around wildly, as if an OBGYN might step forward from behind the dumpster. But of course it's just us. I tell the woman to puff, small breaths, *don't push yet, ma'am*. I'm petrified.

I remember Amy telling me about her first birth on the job. She must have seemed nervous because the woman looked up at her suspiciously and said, "Have you ever done this before?" Amy waved her hands as casually as possible. "No problem," she said in her most soothing Long Islandese. "My dog just had puppies."

Jamie Frank leads the woman carefully over to the bumper of the Rescue rig, and then there is a quiet shuffle as the men step back. This is women's work, they are thinking. But I know nothing about births except what the manual has taught me, a succession of questions and commands that seem far removed from the blood and pain about to happen. Jamie spreads a sheet on the concrete. We lay the woman down as another labor pain comes. She takes this like the first, with a small gasp and open eyes.

"Under a doctor's care?" I ask, kneeling on the sidewalk. The driver, Barney Barret, turns on the searchlight and the wide, gray parking lot disappears, leaving only a pool of light. I notice, in that odd way that peripheral things are noticed when something essential is going on, that the cement glistens as if I kneel on new snow, little winks of silver. I can hear myself breathing in small tight breaths.

Relax, I tell myself, *this has been going on for centuries*. I pick up the scissors and begin to cut her pants off.

I have been to many miscarriages, but those are different. The apartment door opens to clothes tightly wound on the floor, an effort to staunch the insistent rivulet of blood. They lead a frenzied trail to the woman who is often still standing, one hand in her hair, walking in a dazed circle. The only baby I ever saw actually born was miscarried just before we arrived, as the woman was going to the bathroom. It dangled from her, breeched, the small red feet the size of my fingernails.

We birthed it right there and I stared at the tiny creature—four and a half months formed—and thought how I had never seen anything so precise. It was dark blue-red, as if still part of the woman's veins, but she stared at it with distant eyes.

Here the water's broken, the labor pains are less than two minutes apart, and it's a full moon, so a real live birth on the sidewalk seems imminent.

"We took the Greyhound here tonight," the man tells us, "And we're on the way to our hotel." He says no, no drugs, no alcohol. Their doctor says everything's going to be fine, a normal full-term baby. "Due date?" I ask. He tells me it's three weeks away.

The last cut, and the woman's pants fall away. I kneel down, squint, and quickly straighten up.

Jesus, the head is crowning.

"The baby's there," I say, in my calmest, most doctor-like voice, but inside I'm panicking. The officer goes wide-eyed too, then grabs his radio and begins yelling into it, asking why the ambulance is not here yet.

Jamie is already laying the tools out for me: gown, mask, eye bulb, umbilical cord scissors and ties. In the distance a siren begins to wail. Barret the driver walks back over and crosses his arms as if to say *harrumph, can't you women get it together?* But I know that he's interested. It is hard not to be; something miraculous is about to happen. I snap the surgical mask to my face, try to stop my hands from shaking. I glance once more at the moon and think that to be born under it, literally under it, is a powerful talisman. I tell the woman to puff through her lips, to hold on just a little longer. The ambulance screeches around a corner and pulls to a stop.

There is a shuffle and the soft exchange of words—everything is spoken in a low, almost reverent whisper tonight. The two paramedics kneel next to me. I forget that the light blue paper gown over my fire coat looks ridiculous and that I am sweating from anxiety; we are a chorus of pleased smiles.

"Yep," says the tall paramedic, his glasses glinting in the search-light. "No time to transport. We'll just do it right here." He grunts hap-pily, because the fire crew has handled this fine and he too is swept up in the excitement of a birth, even a birth on the sidewalk. His partner taps me on the shoulder. "What do you say, want to give it a go?"

"Me?" I say.

The woman's legs are crooked; her feet are planted on the ground. She has perfect, solid symmetry, the geometry of birth through the ages. The full moon shines, lighting up the "99 cents for a sixpack of Coke" sign that hangs on the wall behind us.

"Yes, you," he says to me, grinning. Then he turns to the others and spreads his hands as if conducting an orchestra. "Okay, we're all ready here, and our little friend especially. At the next labor pain, we want mom to push, all rightey?"

He turns back to me.

"This one is for home plate. Hand on the head, Caroline, gently, so nothing tears too much."

I am anxious—will I remember everything? When the head is free, okay, give a gentle downward pressure to let the shoulder pop out. Got it. Not so difficult, really, just a nudge to let nature do its thing. I nod at the paramedic. He slips a gloved hand into the woman's small palm.

"When the next pain hits, I want you to push with it," I say to the woman, who has her eyes closed now. Her tiny, triangular face looks translucent in the light

Almost immediately, the woman gasps. "Push," I say. "Push." The paramedic leans over to watch.

"Push," he says, and frowns.

The baby's head has not moved. The labor pain hits again, rippling her body enough for her to widen her eyes, and again we exhort her.

"Sarah, you have to push. Push with the pain." The paramedic shifts so that he looms over her small face. The other paramedic, a gaunt man with a lower jaw that juts forward, steps forward.

"Jim, look at this," he says. He holds out something to his partner, and I see it's the woman's underwear that I've just cut off.

Jim stares. He snaps his head to the woman.

"What drug are you on?" he asks. "Don't bullshit me on this one." Without waiting for an answer he shines a light in her eyes.

"Heroin," she says, blinking.

Her underwear is stained green. There is a collective inhale, as if we've all simultaneously been punched in the stomach. Green stains mean only one thing, and that thing is very bad.

"This baby is fucked," the paramedic shouts, spinning around, waving towards the ambulance. "Load and go on this one." Barrett is already moving, yanking open the doors, pulling on the stretcher, wincing as it clatters from its bed. I get up stiffly. The sidewalk has bit into my knees and I feel it now.

We load her quickly. She doesn't say anything, just looks at the sky. Her eyelids close slowly. When they shutter back open, they appear slightly dismayed.

"You too?" I say to the man, bitter. "Heroin?"

"We had some this morning, yeah."

"This morning and tonight."

"Yeah."

"Jesus Christ."

The green stain indicates merconium. Merconium is the baby's first stool, which, if expelled inside the mother, indicates that the infant is in distress. Big distress, possibly fatal.

The paramedics wave us off from the ambulance. They know how much this has taken out of us. We do not say anything to each other as we clean up the remnants of our hastily set-up operating room. Jamie glances at the full moon. I know what he is thinking.

There, that's why.

22.

Danny is a big guy of Irish descent, nice enough, certainly smart, with a long lineage of family in the fire department, a tendency to shout and complain, and remarkably thin skin. This last trait does not go unnoticed in the firehouse. Firefighters soon look for any chance to tease him, just to hear his voice get high and his skin go pink with indignation. This earns him the nickname Pinky, and a long repertoire of good-natured stories about his inability to take a joke.

Which is why today at lunch, Pinky sort of has it coming to him. He likes to run his mouth off, and he is doing it now, this time directing his puffed up ire at the Rescue Squad. "Nobody on that rig can swim," he scoffs, and proceeds to tell the table of his own swimming prowess. He switches again to the Squad, predicting the day when a surf rescue will go terribly awry. As he bloviates, I grow more and more annoyed. This is, after all, my crew and me that he's talking about. But I say nothing. Sometimes someone interjects and this only eggs him on. The crews listen, half amused, half bored. There are other conversations going on, but Danny's is the loudest.

Finally, I lay my fork down, and say, very quietly, "I can swim, Danny."

There is a split second of complete silence.

Then, mayhem.

Laughter, yelling, pounding on the table. "Oooh, Pinky," someone shouts, "Put in your place by a girl!" This migrates quickly into, "She challenged you to a swim-off!" And in no time someone else has leapt from the table and returned with a piece of paper on which is scrawled Swim Duel of the Century and a date, three months hence, when we will face off in the bay. Within an hour it will be all around the department. Caroline and Danny are going to race against each other.

Pinky is up from the table, yelling. "I did not say she couldn't swim," he shouts, his face mottling, his voice desperate. But nobody's listening. They're delighted that Pinky's in a panic. He's pontificated himself into a race that he can never win, because of course a boy can never win against a girl. The best he can do is cross the finish line first and put an end to the saga. The worst is that he can actually lose to her, and then his fate is a life of shame, or hari-kari for the ones who can't take it any more. I almost feel sorry for him, frankly. As the hilarity reaches fever pitch, I stay seated, with a calm half smile on my face. *Sure, sound goods,* my expression says. *A race? Right up my alley.* But inside I'm aghast. I hadn't challenged Danny, nor had he challenged me. Neither of us wants to race, but now it is out of our hands.

The truth is that I *can* swim. My twin and I learned at five and spent every summer on a lake. As children, we went on long swims together, practicing extra for the rinky-dink swim team we were part of until we were teenagers. Throw me in the water now, over 15 years later, and I will still be able to do the freestyle stroke without stopping for miles. Certainly, I am confident that I can rescue people. But a race? No. Danny is going to slaughter me. He has told us many times that he is a triathlon champion in the Heavy, also known as Clydesdale, division, and I know I don't stand a chance.

But I've been in the firehouse long enough to know how to play this game, and so on the outside I stay cool as a cucumber. If I can't win the physical race, at least I can hold fast in the mental one. Within days, firefighters I hardly know ask me how the race is going to go. "Looking forward to it," I say, shaking my arms like I've seen Olympians do poolside, laughing good-naturedly. It is funny. I can see that. But I just wish it wasn't happening to me.

Frantic, I sign up for the master swim program. I rent swim technique videos. I ask a coach to help me on my stroke. I learn the tides and currents of the bay. It doesn't take long to realize I'm going to need more than three months to get into race shape.

Pinky becomes an easy target. In his locker, someone hangs a pink lifejacket. Someone else hangs a photo of my twin in her *Baywatch* suit, holding a buoy. He is told that I was captain of the Stanford swim team (not true) and this rumor quickly gets legs, as all rumors in the firehouse do. He laughs at none of it. Soon he stops speaking to me, as if I am the cause of his distress.

For me things are not going well either. At the masters swim program, 60-year-old women beat me handily during the lap swim. The coach clucks at my swim stroke, proclaiming it badly outdated. "If you throw me in the water I can swim forever," I say hopefully, but the coach looks unimpressed.

Everyone seems to be hoping I'll beat the pants off of Pinky, and quiet his bluster for a while. The men continue to pound him, and it's clear he's slowly unraveling. With a few weeks to go before the race, I'm also cracking, but only my girlfriend, Melea, knows. I hate everything about indoor pools: the soggy air, the goggles that give me a headache, the chlorine, the hours spent staring at a black line. I hate everything about swimming in the bay as well—the frigid temperatures, the oil slick that clings to my face, the murky water. Yes, I'm a little faster, and my stroke has improved by leaps and bounds, but against a triathlete champion, there is no hope. My humiliation looms—I wonder just how far behind I am going to be when Pinky emerges from the water, victorious.

With two days to go, the course is decided and the bets are flying. I seem to be the favorite, which just goes to show that acting low key and confident is a powerful tool. Also, everyone wants to see Danny lose to a girl. But will the department-wide support help me win? No.

The day before the race, the chief walks up to me to make sure that last minute details have been handled. Do I know the course? Yes. Do I have a kayaker lined up to follow me in the event of an issue? Yes. How are you feeling? Good, Chief, really good. Satisfied, the chief phones Danny to check that he is similarly prepared.

"Danny," he says, "Chief here. Just checking that you're set for the race. I need to know."

At this point something seems to happen on the other end of the phone. Those of us at the station can't tell what it is, but we do see the chief's face gets red, then redder. He begins to say Danny's name, not once but twice, then again, and again, louder each time. Finally, the chief slams down the phone. He walks up to me and shouts, "The goddamn race is off."

"What?" I say, shocked, elated.

"It's off. Danny's gone crazy. He's either going to shoot you or himself."

I put on my most morose face. "Really, Chief? I was looking forward to this."

"I'm ordering that we cancel." Then he calls down the rest of the station and tells them the news. "The guy can't handle the pressure," he concludes.

I put on my morose face again, but inside I thank my lucky stars. In my wildest dreams, I didn't think this is the way it would turn out. I had won the mental game, and it turns out to be the one that matters.

I have never seen so much blood. We're slipping and sliding in it. We're windmilling our arms to stay balanced, we're cursing under our breath. The police shine flashlights so the alley lights up, but for now all we have eyes for is the blood. There's nothing so scary, with it's hidden evils of Hep C, Hep B, and HIV, and none of us want to take a spill, so we're gripping tight to the medical bags and lurching inelegantly this way and that. Great viscous pools gleam under the beams, then run in thick rivulets toward us. How much blood can a body hold? Ten pints, I recall, which means five milk containers. Surely, there's more here.

We're sweating by the time we reach the body. We squat down carefully, and take a look. The young man's throat has been slit, ear to ear. This must be where most of the blood is coming from, though he also has deep wounds on both arms, and his penis has been almost completely severed.

"Holy cow," Alberto says under his breath.

We stare in shock for a moment, then Joe growls for us to get a move on. The young man has been stripped of his clothes, which are nowhere in sight.

Nick kneels and puts a hand to the neck and then curses again. "He's alive, goddamn it," and it's miraculous but true—he's breathing shallowly, his eyes are half-closed, and his color is as white as I've ever seen, glowing under the flashlights.

The blood laps up over my boots and I desperately try to find some-place to put the oxygen bag and then I'm bagging him. Blood spurts weakly from the boy's neck. He's half-conscious, gazing at the sliver of night sky between the buildings above us with dreamy eyes. Who the hell did this to you, I want to say, but I don't, because Nick is yelling for an ETA on the ambulance and because this is a load and go, and there's no time for chatter, and the guy is so young, maybe 20, and we want to save him because, well, he's young and anyway it doesn't seem like anyone deserves this kind of violence, this kind of hate.

Two paramedics mince toward us, leaning on their gurney for bal-ance. "The dude's bleeding out," Nick shouts, waving his arms for the backboard, which clatters down next to us into the blood. We roll the victim, check his back then roll him back on the board, quickly secur-

ing him. "Neck, arms, penis, the dude been hacked up," Nick shouts
again as I tell everyone, on three, to lift and we lift and drop the guy on
the gurney and then the paramedics lean in. Nick is dancing at their
shoulder.

"He's breathing, and we got seconds, man, just seconds to save this
fucker."

One of the paramedics whips out a C-collar.

"What're you doing?" Nick screams.

"C-spine precautions," says the paramedic, and starts fiddling with
the Velcro straps and calling for head blocks and tape, the whole shebang. I'm not a paramedic like Nick, but even I can see that this is
stupid, that the guy's dying before our eyes, and who cares that protocol says C-spine goes with neck trauma, who cares, because this kid is
going to die unless he gets to surgery *now*.

"Load and go, load and go!" Nick yells, his finger stabbing at the
air. He's livid, and acting like his Crazy-Nick self in the process, his eyes
bugging out and his face going purple, but the paramedic ignores him
and his partner tells Nick to calm down, it's protocol, to which Nick says
"Fuck protocol." Now we all know what's going on, and even the paramedics look a little sheepish, but they'll be damned if they're going to
wheel this kid into the ER and get yelled at. I've seen it: a doctor chewing out a crew who delivered somebody without a line in the vein, and
it's crazy and it's maddening because the doctors ignore or just don't
understand how it is out here in the field—the screaming bystanders,
the wildly careening ambulance, the terrible lighting, or in this case,
the lake of blood in which we can hardly get a footing. But it doesn't
matter because the paramedics are determined to follow through and
Nick is freaking out as he watches them and Joe, in turn, watches them
all, ready to step in, but only if it's necessary. Alberto and I are swiveling
our eyes from the paramedics, back to Nick, waiting for some direction.

"Load and go, load and go," Nick shouts, jumping up and down
in his fury. I keep bagging but the blood has stopped seeping from

the kid's neck. Nick's right, I know it, but I want the shouting to stop, because it seems like there's been too much violence in this alley for one night anyway, and I know the kid's going to die and I don't want him to hear this all the way to the very end.

"I'm going to write you pussies up," Nick spits.

We finally wheel the gurney to the ambulance and Alberto gets in to help and the rest of us follow in the rig. Nick is so furious he's sputtering, and suddenly I want to hug the guy for so clearly being on the side of the helpless, for being righteously angry, for standing up against rules that make no sense, and for being a little crazy.

The kid dies. Nick has calmed down by then, and we've all changed our uniforms and hosed down our boots. A police officer calls the station for his report and tells us the news. "Gang killing," says Joe in a voice that is only half a question, because we know it's a gang killing, it has to be. This is the Mission District and gang killings are routine. We've just never seen it this vicious.

"No, no," says the police officer. "Sounds crazy, but it was a suicide. That kid took a razor to his dick and his own throat. Hard to believe, right? But he beat his mother to an inch of her life a few hours before, so the guy was a sicko from the first."

"Cut off his own goddamn schlong," Joe tells us in wonderment.

I shake my head. "He did it all to himself?"

We stand there, absorbing this. Death seems to have many permutations, and this is a new one to all of us.

My attitude toward death has changed since the beaten woman on the pier. Back then, and for a while, I imagined that death would always have an existential power over me. So at first I did the corny things: I would lean over the dead person and slowly sweep my hand across their eyelids to close them, as I'd seen done in the movies. But the eyelids would always creep back open, because in real life death takes with it the muscular control to keep them closed, and when I finally realized this, I stopped. If someone died right in front of me, I would glance around surreptitiously, hoping to glimpse whatever essence was now departing. I imagined it wispy and light, leaving a faint trail of something like cigarette smoke. I would nod a quiet farewell, so no fire-fighter could see. But that was then. Now, death has become mundane. What occupies me more is the suffering the person endured in life.

"How can you actually ..." I mime taking a knife across my own throat. I shiver. The hate and violence in that alley had not come from a gang. It had come from someone's own self-loathing.

"I know," says Joe.

"C-spine was still bullshit," Nick murmurs.

23.

Chief Kalafferty listens the way most firefighters listen; his head is cocked to one side and he nods occasionally or leans in closer. He is not the chief on my shift, but he is the chief on duty today, and the matter is urgent. There's no time to wait.

"I'll need to borrow an engine. Just for an hour." I look off to the left to make sure no one else hears. "The television show says that without it, they have no story. I know that's not true but..."

"So it's for your brother. He's in jail." There is no mockery in the chief's voice. He is a tall man whom I do not know well, and despite his thoughtful attention I am suddenly scared that I have done the wrong thing. Hat in hand, I am asking a tremendous favor. He may break out in wild laughter, for all I know, and kick me out of his office.

"He's in jail, but he is not guilty of anything," I blurt out—yeah, right, isn't that what everyone says? "I mean, truly, he hasn't done anything and they say he hasn't ..." I finish lamely. I sound crazy even to myself. Even my liberal friends do not understand the grand jury system. Why should Chief Kalafferty?

My brother has been in jail for six months. Finally, we have decided to take a different course of action to try to free him. Reluctantly, Alexandra and I concede that good old American protest procedures are not working. We have simply frozen the ends of our fingers and gone through many D cell batteries for our small, cheap megaphone. We have become recognizable figures in Spokane, as a local drunk might be. Otherwise, not much has changed. Jonathan remains in jail.

The letters that we have sent to *The New York Times*, to *60 Minutes*, to the ACLU and elsewhere have focused only on the injustices of the grand jury. We have written long, passionate polemics on the sanctity of the Constitution. We have expounded on the right to free speech, waxed poetic about the proud history of political activity, and pondered sternly a country without them. In return, we receive thoughtful letters that agree, yes, the grand jury is a suspect institution that needs scrutiny. But right now, they add regretfully, there are more urgent situations to consider. Sorry.

Finally, we realize we haven't been hard hitting enough. Who cares about the Constitution? What's the big deal about the threat of government intrusion on innocent citizens? There is something even more mesmerizing than our inalienable rights, and we know what it is. Reluctantly, we play our trump card.

Baywatch.

Baywatch Beauty Bemoans Brother Behind Bars! The television shows and newspapers that had ignored our earlier press releases now snap to attention. Within hours, *People* magazine and *Entertainment Tonight* have called. *The San Francisco Examiner*, *Hard Copy*, *USA Today*, and the *Sally Jesse Raphael* talk show are not far behind. *Fire engines and bathing suits*! they clamor. *What a story*! they cheer. *Baywatch Babe and Fire Girl Team up for Real Life Rescue*!

"Your brother is in trouble," the chief says again. He knows nothing of the press hullabaloo that twenty-four hours from now will make me a semi-recognizable face in my own right for just about another twenty-four hours. "Of course. Take the engine. This has to go through channels, to the chief of the department, but I'll handle it." He pats me on the shoulder. I stare, dumbfounded, as he walks away. I know how much he has just done for me.

Until this point, I have told nobody in the fire department that my brother is in jail, and that we are desperately trying to get him out. But now the television shows are asking that I drive a fire engine for their cameras. I respond with a vigorous, no, there is no way I am going to inform the fire department of this personal matter. But Alexandra has come forward, putting her career on the line. I know I am being a coward.

So I call Patricia. She listens in silence to my fractured voice and convoluted story.

Finally she says, "It's not about being a stupid liberal, Caroline. This is about family. It's about getting your brother out of jail. Of course you have to do this. And if there is anything a firefighter understands, it's family. I guarantee that you will get that engine. So stop being a chickenshit, and ask for it."

Sure enough, as I watch the receding back of Chief Kalafferty, I think how I have once again been embraced by the fire department when I least expect it. To drive a fire engine, off duty and in front of the media, is a big favor indeed. The fire department has strict guidelines about its representation in the media. The media, after all, has often portrayed the fire department in the worst of light. In other instances, it doesn't give the department any credit at all.

Recently, for example, the newspapers reported the heroism of a passerby who caught a baby thrown from a burning building, an event worthy of a feature story. However, not mentioned at all was the fact that four other children were also saved, pulled out of that same fire by Rescue 2. When I arrived at work the next day and heard about it, I hunted them down, hungry for the story. I found William first. He shook his head slowly.

"It was the other guys," he said. "I just followed them."

Then I found Jamie Frank, who peered at me from behind his glasses. "I just helped," he murmured. "The others are the real heroes."

"It was pretty satisfying," the officer said. "But you should get the story from the rest of the crew. I didn't do much." And so on. Since the newspaper had not bothered to cover it, I never did find out much about the rescue.

Today, however, the media is interested. From my perch on the driver seat of the engine, I can just make out the nose of a television camera in a van next to me. The producer leans out the van's front window, which keeps pace with me, and shouts above the wind.

"Yeah, look straight ahead. You know, as if you are going on a rescue. Perfect, perfect. Okay, let's get your face a little towards me now, but keep driving. Serious, but not solemn. You know, you are speeding to rescue your brother, speeding to get him out of jail..."

It is hard to get just the right angle of face for the camera while driving at a decent speed and simultaneously praying that no one I know will come by.

"How about the emergency beacon?" the producer waves at me.

Shit. I flip the lights on.

"Yeah, good, perfect!" shouts the producer, and we speed on down the wide, quiet street.

Within twelve hours of that absurd fire engine drive, my brother is out of jail. The feds say that it has nothing to do with the sudden avalanche of press interest. They say that it is clear that he was not being "persuaded," that he would never testify, and that it was time to let him go. My fellow firefighters do not ostracize me for my family's political bent. There is no shame in having a brother in jail. "How's your brother?" they ask, genuinely curious, genuinely concerned.

Woman hit by a train, announces the loudspeaker. Jesus, we groan, and head to the rig. A woman hit by a train is not a pleasant call; blood, guts, *parts* everywhere.

"She's about two cars back," a shaken conductor tells us. "Two cars back, *underneath*." The commuter train, he says, was pulling into the station when she jumped onto the tracks in front of it. He jammed on the brakes, he said, but it was too late to do anything but look away.

"That third rail turned off?" My probation officer, Captain Leahy, is here too. It's good to see him again. His large loping stature and deep voice calm the conductor, who wipes a hand along his mouth and looks terribly pale. The third rail carries the voltage to power the train. Turned on, it will electrocute anyone who touches it. It runs a little lower than a knee high along the wall next to the far tracks, a thick, ominous girder of metal.

Even when the all clear is given, everyone remains nervous. We all know an unwitting employee at a central computer may throw the switch back on, activating the third rail while the body recovery process is in progress.

"You ain't catching me going under that thing," someone from Engine 82 murmurs.

It does look forbidding. The snub nose of the forward car hunkers impassively on the tracks. The cars are long. To get to the body, we must crouch and crawl under the space between the platform and the first rail. We will lug our medical equipment—oxygen, bandages, neck braces—but we know this is being optimistic. Two cars ran over her— there won't be much left. Blood and guts will be everywhere. When we get closer, we will confer, and send somebody under the train. If necessary, we'll use the Rescue Squad's hydraulic air bags, and lift the train off of the corpse.

Halfway down the first car, waddling and crawling single file with the Squad and fellow Station 64 members, some of whom are not exactly lithe, we hear a noise.

Oh for goodness sake, I think, *she's half-alive.*

We duck to look under the train. We can't see anything; there just isn't much room. The thinnest of us will have to go in, and that means me. Even I can't get through with my gear on, so I shed my turnout coat and helmet. I snap on medical gloves, my only protection now. Two pair on each hand. Butted together like cattle, it is hard to move, but Jamie Frank manages to reach over and pat my shoulder.

When somebody loses an eyeball, a small Dixie cup will do. Tape it to the bad eye, which can then dangle protected. Then be sure to cover the good eye. If the good eye remains uncovered it will swivel, and thereby swivel the bad eye in unison. I think of the Dixie cup now, small and waxy with flowers along its edges, a solution so neat and practical as to be almost beautiful. But there will be more than an eyeball to worry about here. There will be legs and arms and hands. A Dixie cup cannot help now.

I wriggle over the first rail. I can feel the ribs of the train against my back, the ribs of the rail against my stomach. I am a modern day Jonah, trapped inside this huge, many-ton whale, crawling towards a newly digested victim. Irrational thoughts suddenly spring up in my head: what if the train suddenly moves? What if the Big One happens right now? What if the third rail is really on?

"Get me the hell out of here," says a thin voice in front of me.

I stop to listen. Surely that was my imagination. Surely, no one under here could be alive. Except for my loud breath, I don't hear anything. I squeeze past another network of pipes and coils. "Get me the motherfuck out of this place." And there she is, lying perfectly still, seemingly intact.

"My head hurts like a motherfucker," she says as I get to her.

Oh Christ, I whisper. *Oh Christ.*

The woman has her hands folded across her chest. She stares straight up at the underbelly of the train and does not turn her head even as I reach out to touch her shoulder. She is thin, slightly bedraggled, in her late twenties—though it is hard to tell much in the subterranean light.

She is an inch or so from the wheels of the train on the second rail. The third rail is a foot to her left and right above her.

She is completely unharmed.

I had been expecting terrible carnage, severed parts and a lot of blood. There was certain death on both sides—not including the fact that the train hit her as well. But she fell, perfectly centered, while two train cars passed over her, in the only trough that could have saved her life.

"Do you believe in God?" I ask. "Because you will now."

"My head hurts," she says in response.

Extricating her is a slow process. She stares straight up almost the whole time. She is drunk, and maybe high, which accounts for both her stupidity and for the fact that she is alive in spite of it.

"I wanted to cross the tracks," she says, as the stretcher is pushed towards me and I ask her what the heck she was doing, anyway. "I just wanted to get across." You're kidding, I think. You're kidding, right? She repeats it again, she wanted to cross the tracks, as if I'm the one who's dumb and just doesn't get it.

Life is short. Miracles happen. These are the pithy truisms you think after a call like this one. You laugh, shake your head, make the call into a fire story, which isn't hard because it's already unbelievable. But inside you know: second chances are miracles, and life is too short for loose ends.

My mother is the loosest of the loose ends. Aside from courtesy calls at holidays, we do not speak much. She has made more effort in the past years, but I am slow to respond. It's hard to shake the immature teenager inside me, even now that I'm in my thirties. She's dogged, rearing up in conversations she doesn't belong, tapping my shoulder to remind me of past hurts that no longer apply. She's long served her usefulness as watchdog and protector, but she refuses to leave when it comes to my mother. But second chances are not often given. Today, it is hard not to see the miracle in a woman run over by a speeding train and yet still unharmed.

Today I tell the teenager in me to go to hell.

I pick up the phone. I clear my throat.

"I just wanted to say hello," I tell my mother.

24.

I check the chore board to see if I cook today—no, it is Paul's turn. The meal will be good, though in the middle of dinner Paul will frown and shake his head. "Needs more, more *something*," he will sigh. "Something. I'm not sure what." He will remain forlorn and slightly puzzled at each bite for the rest of the meal.

I hear a *click, click* behind me and Chief Masters walks by, his bicycle shoes tap-dancing across the linoleum. He bikes 25 miles to work if the weather is right and recently on his 56th birthday he biked those 25 miles home and straight to a triathlon, where he handily won in his age group and came in fourth overall. He waves a good morning to me and the rear view mirror on his helmet bobs up and down. He has been in the department for thirty years, and has taken all the changes with good humor.

Of course, traditions die hard. I once found a hayfork in the bowels of Truck 53. The tiller operator shrugged when I held it up to him. He said it was used long ago when the horses were here (and as the last horses retired in 1921, it was a very long time ago). No one had bothered to remove it. "It's good for stuff," he said vaguely, and we put it back. Tradition is both the cornerstone and the lodestone of the San Francisco Fire Department.

But change is the law of life, and transition is difficult. Things have certainly changed since I first got in five years ago. There are eighty women firefighters now. It does not seem a lot on the surface—still only five percent of the department—but it's a startling change from the mere fifteen or so when I began. They come from fancy colleges, too: Brown, Georgetown, Reed. I am no longer an anomaly. When once I might not see another female firefighter for months, now it is not uncommon for me to have another woman on my shift, and today there is a probationer from Station 72.

Cristine Prentice is a short, stocky woman with a flat top of graying hair. I do not know her well because she works on a different shift and because Truck 72, housed here temporarily while their house is under construction, is miserable at Station 64, and spends as much time away as possible. They are set to leave in a few months, and they've begun a gleeful countdown.

Cristine does not wear her nose ring at work, nor can you always see the tattoo on her left upper arm, but she shows it when I ask. It is a beautiful tattoo, with an intricate, artistic pattern. As I stare at it, I realize that it is made of Chinese characters.

"Mandarin," she says.

"What does it say?"

"It's better to die on your feet than to live on your knees," she answers.

Despite her tattoo, and her tough, butch appearance, Cris is anything but hard-edged. I had seen her once at a fire, while she waited to be accepted into the academy, gazing wistfully at the smoke and the firefighters. A part of me wanted to scoff *get a life*, but another part of me was pleased. Women, it seemed, could be fire geeks too.

Now she is an eager probationer, and walks around with the contained glee of someone whose dream has come true. It is not often, I think, that dreams come true.

"Had a fire yet?" I ask.

She shakes her head mournfully.

"It'll come."

"Not soon enough."

"Hmm," I say, nonchalant, a little haughty. I'm not a vet, but I'm not a probie, and the idea of a first fire seems distant.

Cris will get the quiz, much like the one Patricia gave me. This "quiz" is just an informal run-through that clues the new female probationer in fire etiquette. Don't Give Up Your Equipment. Be aggressive. Don't talk about being scared. Usually, I mention these things when the woman first arrives, but Cris is not on my shift. I will wait until after her first fire, I think, and see whether she is as tough as her tattoo.

The driver from Truck 72 waves for Cris; they're going on a drill. Usually they leave and stay out awhile, but now they're no longer allowed to sneak by their station to check on the work in progress, because the contractors have complained to the city. They don't like the way the men stand with their arms crossed, squinting at the exposed joists, or put their hands on a wall seam and frown, or harrumph through the shattered dormitory, commenting on the placement of the pole holes.

Truck 72's impatience to return to their own station is understandable. The Mission can be a depressing place. New yuppie bars have sprung up since I began working here, and eclectic cafes squeeze themselves between popular burrito places, but the sleazy, rundown hotels and the two housing projects in our first alarm area remain.

A fire in the projects is a tricky event. Because the buildings are made mostly of concrete, fire does not spread easily, but the concrete walls act as an oven would, so a burning apartment quickly becomes unbearably hot. Backdrafts or flashovers are a concern. A flashover is when the room gets so hot that objects reach their ignition temperature and combust, without direct contact with flame. A backdraft is different; here, a fire in an enclosed room will begin to produce partially combusted carbons or carbon monoxide instead of carbon dioxide. Carbon monoxide is extremely explosive at a certain range when mixed with air. This is why ventilation is imperative as early as possible. Ventilation—breaking windows, opening up the roof—will prevent carbon monoxide from building up to its explosive range. But it is also why incorrect ventilation—which will actually introduce the air required for a backdraft—is dangerous. Optimally, ventilation will be done early and above the fire so that air will not mix with carbons. But often a door must be opened to get to the fire or a window blows out from the heat and air enters below the fire. It then rises to meet the carbon monoxide, creating an explosion. Fire has scientific properties, but firefighters do not always have the time or the group coordination to be scientific.

My few fires in the projects have been quick, hot affairs. Mostly, the garbage chute catches fire—this is especially unpleasant. Sometimes tenants ignore the garbage chute and simply throw their trash into a lightwell. After one such lightwell fire, I stood on the top of the garbage, two stories high, and raked through it with an axe to make sure that nothing was still burning. Suddenly I was sure that the mound was moving. But no, it wasn't moving. The roaches in it were moving. Flushed by the fire, they now ran up and down the walls in packs. I'm not squeamish, but that day it took all the discipline I had not to catapult myself off the garbage flapping my coat sleeves and emitting girlish yelps.

We rarely expect a large fire in the projects because there is little way for it to spread easily; however, a full box there remains ominous and unpredictable. Just a few years ago, several San Francisco firefighters were burned and one firefighter died in what was initially considered a normal "room and contents" project fire. The fire was started by a young boy playing with a lighter. When the crews arrived, they lined the narrow dark hallway outside the apartment. There was not much smoke, and little reason to worry, or so they thought. They forced open the door. A stiff wind that day pushed the fire toward the front of the apartment, meeting the firefighters as they entered. Flame and superheated air engulfed them.

At the funeral for Lieutenant Manner, who died of his burns more than a week later, my friend, Kathy, still had her ears bandaged. Others had hands wrapped or could not attend from leg burns. What had started as a routine full box ended in tragedy. We are told to expect the unexpected, but sometimes the unexpected is cloaked in mundane reality. An easy room-and-contents turns and kills without sentiment.

Sometimes, if the alarm comes in the dead of night, I push myself up from sleep as if fighting a gravitational pull not experienced during the day. Though my body feels leaden and unresponsive, I am able to get into my turnout pants, slide down the pole and into the rig as if an unknown force guides me. If I am driving, I snap awake as I turn the key and the engine roars to life; if I am not, it sometimes takes the bright lights of an apartment or the grinning of a wide, bloody wound to shake the dullness from me. Fortunately, over the years, waking quickly and efficiently countless times in one night has become a normal part of my sleep pattern. Even at home I wake suddenly and for no apparent reason, alert and listening.

But tonight the lights in the dormitory snap on and seem to pin me to the bed. The Bee-Bop tone wraps around my head and yanks it sideways. The loudspeaker shouts an address I do not recognize at first through my haze, but I am already perched on the side of the bed as if I know that it is for me and the Squad. I shake my head to clear it and my suspenders are on my shoulders before I realize that every rig in the house is going—a full box at the nearby projects.

The flames shoot out of a fifth floor window. Joe leads, nodding at Chief Masters as he passes. No one tells us what to do. We already know.

Behind me, Alan takes the stairs two at a time. Alan is easygoing and polite; he would not ordinarily push past me. But this is a fire, and all etiquette is out the window. He and I reach the fifth floor, he first by half a floor, both of us out of breath. The hallway is filling with smoke. We plunge down it, turn right, and here the smoke thickens. A woman crouches, coughing, near an open doorway.

"Anyone in there?" Joe shouts, as Alan and I kneel at the threshold and pull our masks on.

"My grandson," she cries.

Joe, who is always in a calm, steady motion, stops suddenly, and spins around.

"He's in there? Your grandson?"

"No! Maybe..." The woman looks around confused.

"Hey, we've got him," someone behind her says, "He's right here," but Alan has already plunged into the apartment. He goes to the left, so I go to the right, crawling, patting, straining wildly to see something in the thick smoke. The rasp of my air mask is loud and the air is hot. Like an oven, I think. Like a long molten tube into the center of the earth.

I spread my arms wide along the ground. Every few seconds I reach with my flashlight and tap the wall to make sure I keep my orientation, miss no rooms or closets and break windows as they come up. I know that these apartments are small. I know that my crew is somewhere nearby. But in the dark, the room seems fathomless; despite the hard objects I keep running into, I feel that I might be falling.

I break a window with a quick tap of my flashlight. So far, no one here. The room goes from pitch black to cooler murky gray. Goodbye, carbons. You have not gotten us today.

I continue crawling, searching, my flashlight trickling a weak light, the smoke escaping faster now. I am back around to the left, where Alan disappeared, and where the fire is. I hear the clamor of the engine crew advancing a line. Then there's a rush of water, everything cools, and I lurch from the room.

Joe is right behind. Alan is there already, crouching by the door. "Where's the kid?" he snaps. "I didn't find the kid."

He makes a move to re-enter the apartment, but Joe puts a hand on his shoulder. Alan's helmet is bent and blistered. Jesus Christ. He was so close to the fire his helmet has melted. He does not notice, though it is easy to smell, the sharp tang of paint. He wants to find the kid.

"Don't worry," Joe says. "They say he's out. Can I see the kid?" he asks the grandmother again, who has retreated, dull-eyed, only a few feet from the door. "I got him," says a young man behind her, and indeed a small scared-looking boy clutches the man's legs. Joe walks toward him. I know what he is doing—he wants to know for certain that no one is dead in there, and he needs to lean in and see the kid for himself so that no mistakes are made. He needs to know why he plunged into that hot-as-hell apartment. Since that question is not easily answered, he needs to see something tangible and real—that the grandson is here and all right. Joe leans towards the little boy.

He brushes the young man's arm with his dirty turnout coat.

"Hey," the man says. "Hey, motherfucker. You got my shirt dirty."

"Sorry, buddy, I just need to talk to the kid."

"My motherfucking shirt's dirty." The man looks incredulously at his sleeve and brushes it slowly with one hand. Joe, who has just risked his life for the young man's nephew, pushes by again.

"I said, get the fuck away from me, motherfucker. You're getting my shirt dirty."

Joe turns slowly towards the man. I am frozen in place, disbelieving. Alan has straightened up. There is a moment of thick, tense silence.

Joe raises one arm, his sleeve wet and dirty, and points past the man's nose.

"Then get outta the fucking hallway," he says.

"It's my hallway," is the louder response.

Suddenly everything that just happened is torn away. We are not rescuers, but white people in uniforms, and he, a black man, hates us once again. Here are the signs of a backdraft—the partially combusted carbons in the air in the form of our old prejudices, the heat generated

by the small swipe of dirt on a coat, and now we are just waiting for
the slight breath of oxygen to slide in and ignite the place into flames.

I pick up the young boy, who is crying now, and turn him away
from the fight about to happen. This diverts the man, who jerks his
head towards me. "Give me my nephew," he says.

"I'm just going to take him to the ambulance," I stammer.

"Put my nephew down," the man says stepping forward.

"It's fine, really," I say. I'm never articulate under stress (someone
stole my parking space once, and all I could squeak out was, "You're
mean,") and today is no exception.

"For the kid," I say lamely, making no sense except to myself. What
I mean is: do we have to do this in front of a five year old? Does the
cycle of distrust, miscommunication and racial discord have to continue here, when we're all tired, maybe scared, certainly oversaturated
with adrenalin? If we do this now, in a tight hallway full of grimy
smoke, with a fire still smoldering nearby, is there any hope for any of
us, any of us at all?

Instead I back away, mumbling, and suddenly the tension is dif-
fused, perhaps because I've confused everyone. No one looks like
they're going to hit each other anymore, and they watch us leave.

In front of the building I hand the boy to Chief Masters.

"What's your name, little guy?" The white veteran asks the small
black boy in his arms. I watch as the boy wipes his eyes, then says something. Masters nods. Then the boy shyly lifts one hand. In it is a small,
yellow, plastic toy. I can't make out what it is. Masters reaches for it and
holds it up to the streetlight.

They both admire the toy silently. I step back, then walk quietly
away. I hear the two murmuring, and I imagine Masters somberly asking how it works, and the little boy, just as earnest, explaining.

25.

The room is smoky, but not too bad. I can still see my hand in front of my face and the dim outline of my officer. This is our third room. So far, nobody.

My officer disappears into a closet and when he reappears he has a dog in his arms. It is mid-size, almost all black, and I'm duly impressed that he has found him in the deteriorating conditions.

"Take him out," my officer orders and drops the dog into my arms. The dog doesn't struggle. He seems in shock.

I talk to the dog the whole way down the stairs, through the front door, down the next set of stairs, and onto the sidewalk. I have my mask on, so most of it is garbled, but I'm sure the dog gets the gist. Animals do. I scan the crowd of gawkers for a paramedic but instead see an off-duty firefighter. I call her over.

"Ambulance, oxygen," I say, handing the dog to her, ruffling his fur once he lands in her arms, telling him he's a good dog, that this is Connie, that she'll take good care of him.

Back inside the smoke has gotten worse, and word is that the fire had spread to two exposures. Soon I have to go out again, to change my air bottle. I do this fast, then jog back toward the fire.

Connie suddenly appears before me. "There's another one," she says, breathless. Momentarily I am confused. What? "The owners say there's two dogs," she says.

I look at her, then at the black smoke streaming out of the holes in the roof. "Shit," I say, angry at the owners for not telling anyone sooner, angry at myself for failing in my initial search. I head back inside.

The first animal I ever saved bit me. When I still held on, he dropped two panicked turds onto my turnout coat. I didn't blame him; it had been a bad doggy day. Flames, smoke, heat. He and I made our way out to fresh air, and there was the owner, arms outstretched, crying. I wanted to lean into the dog's soggy terrier ear and tell him how honored I was to rescue him, and sorry for the rough handling, but she had grabbed him and buried her face into his fur.

I come from a long lineage of animal rescuers. My father gave mouth-to-mouth resuscitation to three wild ducklings who had been sucked into his pool filter. The mother duck flapped frantically while my father, genuflecting on the hard cement, tried to remember first aid. I can see him now, hands cupped around the still mounds of feathers, putting small puffs of air into tiny beaks.

My brother was suspended from high school because of a clandestine operation to free mice from glue traps. He spent hours sneaking through buildings, carefully extracting the exhausted, suffering creatures. He recruited friends to fish the glue traps from the dumpsters into which they had been tossed, mice still alive and attached. If the mice were too far gone, he tried to give them quick, painless deaths.

My job is easier. There is no wild mother duck pecking at my back. No mice necks to snap. Just crawl in the dark. Murmur encouraging sounds through the air mask. Grab the scruff, wrestle if necessary. Embrace and soothe. Make for the exit.

Honestly though, there is little wrestling. Even the cats seem to realize I'm here to help. At one fire, I approached a cat from the far end of the room, sure she was going to run away despite the soothing noises

I was trying to make, the telepathic message that I was trying to send. She watched me lumber toward her in full fire gear, the rasp of my breath in the mask surely sounding like some terrible predator. But she didn't run. She let me pick her up and press her against my rough turn-out coat and cart her out. She, like the others, seemed to understand that while I was clumsy, ugly and loud, I was her best bet for survival.

I once saw a kitten on a window ledge, four stories up, that had fled a fire and the resulting sprinkler system. I raced up the stairs, pushed past the crowd of firefighters in the fire room, paused at the window, took a breath, and leaned slowly out. There she was, bedraggled, petrified, the size of my palm, almost more than an arm length away, but not quite, not yet. Afraid she might run or fall, I reached as slowly as my adrenalin allowed, cooed quietly, thought cat thoughts, leaned as far as I could, pinched her scruff and brought her inside. I almost wept with relief, then dried her as best I could with my t-shirt, dropped her into my coat and pushed my way back outside.

On the other end of the spectrum is the German Shepherd I carry out a few months later. He is a huge animal, and I hold him awkwardly, with legs askew and his head pressed against my forearm, but he just looks at me thoughtfully as we step over broken glass and charred wood. He does not at any time growl or bare his teeth. "Lady," he seems to be saying. "Thanks for the help. Even though you're killing my neck."

But could a dog survive in this smoke? I race up the stairs and back into the building. I'm going to have to find her fast, but where could she be? It must be somewhere good, if we missed her the first time. *Think like a dog,* I tell myself, and I reach the landing and stop. *Think like a dog.* And then it hits me like a flash. Of course I know where the dog is.

Dogs are pack animals. Dogs are loyal animals. Dogs stay together.

I find the closet again. This time I push aside all the clothes on the rack and then dig into all the clothes on the floor. Finally the beam of my flashlight, cutting weakly through the smoke, catches her eyes, and they gleam momentarily, and there she is, jet black, all but invisible. I drag her toward me and she struggles briefly but I pull her into my lap, hold her firmly for a moment, and think alpha dog thoughts. She calms. I clumsily stand. It's then that she sags in my arms with something like utter trust. Later I realize it was probably simply utter resignation, but it doesn't change the moment, when something luminescent passes between us. We are two different creatures, but our lives are intersecting, fleetingly, profoundly. I quickly walk out, and at the stairwell, I see a new, young firefighter. "Can you take this dog?" I say. The firefighter beams, reaches out, cradles the dog carefully, and walks with her into the day.

26.

The second alarm comes in near midnight. William is driving today and because the fire is in Hunter's Point, we take the freeway. The Squad shakes and groans from the strain of going so fast. I put on gloves, stiff from ash and dirt, and hold my hands in front of me to flex them. Coat, belt, helmet—they are all in place. Now all I can do is sit and wait.

The Squad lunges onto the sidewalk and noses to a halt. William and I are partners tonight, which is funny because both of us have been separately reprimanded for "freelancing": when you suffer from impatience and aggressiveness and tend to leave your partner behind. In fact, the best firefighters are the ones who pause, consider the situation, make a decision, and communicate it to everyone else. Freelancing is understandably frowned upon. It is not only stupid, egotistical and often ineffectual, it is also dangerous. Tonight, both William and I are on our best behavior.

I don't see flames, but the house, a two-story family residence, is haloed in orange light. The sky is blurry with smoke. We throw a quick salute to a chief who stands in the middle of the street, a radio pushed against his ear. It is hard to hear anything above the shouts for more water, more ladders, more axes. Hoses lie everywhere and water sprays through leaks in couplings. Fire vehicles jam the street.

"Rescue 2 is here, Chief," William says.

"Okay, we got a report of two people still in the back room," the chief answers matter-of-factly, unfolding himself from the radio. "A baby and an adult."

Pause, look, I say to myself as I walk quickly towards the fire. *Be as matter-of-fact as he is.* The chief is not unfeeling; he simply knows that the tone of his voice will affect the adrenalin level in his firefighters. *Pause, look,* I tell myself again, but instead the word BABY pounds in my head.

The garage door, at street level, is twisted and burned. Smoke cartwheels from the opening and two hose lines disappear into the darkness. "Front door," I breathe to William and bound up the steps. There is already a hose snaking its way inside—an engine company's attack.

My mask is on and I turn to make sure that William has followed me inside. I do not want to lose him or be lost by him; tonight we need to do everything perfectly. Instead, a civilian has followed me, and he is wringing his hands and pointing. There is black all over his face, and I wonder if he has been burned. He grabs my coat as if to shake me; I see that he is crying—perhaps he has grabbed me to steady himself. I cannot understand a word he says—he looks Cambodian—but I know what is going on. It is his baby inside, in the back room.

I take both his shoulders to prevent him from going further, and he becomes frantic. He sobs and points to the far wall of the house. By this time, William is past me and on the opposite side of the room, where flashlights and dim outlines of helmets appear—the engine crew. They have not made much headway, and something has stopped them at a small hall.

I push the man back as gently—as *matter-of-factly*—as I can and join William. It is hot, very hot. We need to get through, I say, there are two people in the back.

"Stay back," hisses the rear firefighter, whom I do not recognize in the darkness. "We got this handled."

"There are two people in the back," I begin again.

"Stay back!" and this time he swings his arm around to push us away.

William is trying hard to keep his voice calm. "Look, we don't want the nozzle. We're the Squad and there are people trapped."

"Don't push us forward," the large man screams, and the urgency in his voice makes me step away.

I quickly check an adjacent room but there is no access to any other place. Am I missing a door in the dark? Is there a stairway I have not seen? I grab the Cambodian father.

"Is there any other way to the back?"

He points frantically again to the far wall of the room amid a hail of indistinguishable words. "Any-other-way," I repeat in that exaggerated, idiotic way that people try to speak through language barriers. Then I drop his shoulders and say. "Don't worry, I promise." His eyes pin mine. I push him away from the smoke and darkness towards the outside.

When he has been dragged to the front door, William and I fly down the stairs. We dive into the garage. As my air hose gets caught on the bumper of a car, William melts into the dark ahead of me. Shit, I think. That freelancer. He's gone. I disentangle myself and crawl further in. Near the front wheel, William reappears. "Can't get through! All bunched up!" he yells.

"The rear. Get to the rear," I answer, and we take off again, holding each others' coat sleeves, each pulling the other out of habit, out of impatience, out of urgency.

The way to the back has already been trampled by axes, chainsaws and well-aimed kicks. The neighbors say nothing as we follow the destruction through their house, out their yard and through the yawning hole of what was once a neat, tall fence. The smoke in the back is thick, but I can just make out a window above me. But the whole bottom of the house roils in flame. How can we get to that window?

Someone grabs my shoulder and I turn to see another chief, his white helmet gleaming against the flames, beckoning. "There's a lady here who's jumped, we need the Squad to help her." Several firefighters surround a ghostly white face. Simultaneously, William reaches and jumps at a fence that lines the other side of the yard. I grab a foot and a knee and push him up. He teeters at the top and then shimmies to a small roof next to the burning building. I grab a chainsaw and pass it up to him. He's going to cut through the wall, to gain entrance into the building.

The chief pulls at me again. "Chief," I say, "we're going in for someone else." He melts away, understanding.

I pull myself up on the fence. Someone, the chief it seems, pushes me the last few inches.

"Christ," William mutters. "This roof won't hold." He is balanced precariously on a plastic greenhouse-like structure, but manages to start the chainsaw anyway. By now I have his belt buckle to steady him, and I crouch on the fence like a gymnast new to the balance beam. "Shit," William yells suddenly above the whine. "The damn wall is metal." He revs the saw and tries to cut through it anyway, to no avail.

The window is a good five feet away, to my left, but I think I might make it if I jump and grab enough sill. "No way," shouts William. "Then I can't back you up in there." He is right, but I know that left to his own devices he would consider the same thing, and if anyone could do it, he could. I feel more frantic than I want to. I can still see the father's wide eyes and his stretched, grief-stricken face.

Another eight feet away bordering the greenhouse roof is a second-floor window into a different house. *If we can make it across the flimsy plastic roof by stepping on the wooden beams...*

William treads carefully and reaches the window. I follow him, but I am less careful. When the roof gives way I am not thinking that I may get hurt, but that I may not be able to keep my promise to the crying father. At the last second I wedge my arms out and catch myself on the beams. I hang there for a moment while William calls out, "Are you okay?" I assure him I am fine, that I am going to lower myself and climb back up. Meanwhile, I think about the weight I am wearing. Air pack, turnout coat, crash ax, flashlight—fifty or so pounds extra. I hear the anguish in William's voice. *Are you okay*, he keeps saying over and over, unable to see me well in the dark and smoke. I tell him to go on ahead, that there is nothing he can do on this thin, uncertain roof, that I can handle this and meanwhile scream to myself *You Idiot*! I carefully half-slither, half-drop to the ground. There I crouch and quickly assess myself. Nothing broken, just a bruise or two and this tight chest, this pounding heart. Suddenly, my world has narrowed to the dim outline of a baby's body. I look once at the sky, murmur something that sounds like a prayer, and force myself back up the fence. When I am on the roof again, this time I move gingerly, around the gaping hole I have just made, muttering advice to myself to step slowly, *here, there, now*. When I reach the window, William hauls me in.

A woman—clearly the neighbor—rushes in when she hears the sound of the chainsaw. She is aghast when I unceremoniously tip her side table over to make room. William waves for her to step back, his large dark eyes wide, and swings the blade into the wall.

The hole seems to take forever to cut, but it can only be a minute, not longer. I pull at the lathe and plaster with my crash axe while William pushes the blade through one house and into the next. I can only think of the small body of a baby waiting on the other side, waiting for this act of desperation to reach her. The woman has backed into a corner and then out the door as if somehow the very posture of us has told her not to try to interfere, even though we are here without so much as a Hello, I'm Caroline and this is William and we need to destroy your house as a last ditch effort, do you mind?

I drop my air pack. I scramble to get into the hole. Suddenly, the long beam of a flashlight hits my eyes. *Fuck*, I hiss, and almost collapse with exhaustion back into the room.

"They're there," I manage to say, leaning against the wall. "They got the fire out and they're getting into the room." William turns away, head down. He lets the saw drop onto the queen-size bed, once neat, but now covered with lathe, plaster and wood chips.

The body is found a few minutes later. It's a four-year-old boy, and he was never in the room we were trying to get into, but at the bottom of the stairs two floors down, in the burning garage. This should be some sort of consolation, but it isn't.

Instead I rake through all the furniture in that back room methodically, and I do not believe that the kid is not there until William points out the small, disintegrating body, like a cashew left in an ashtray, in the garage below us.

I lean against the wall. Could we have saved him? Did I make a wrong step, a wrong turn, a wrong decision? I want to put my head down and weep, partly from exhaustion, partly from the shock of failure. I think of the father, and his frantic gestures. He had looked to me to save the most important thing in his life and I had failed.

There is a crowd outside the front door. I head to the rig, in shock. Off to the left, three people huddle together. A small Cambodian woman is in the middle. To her right is a man who has slung an arm around her and wrapped himself into her. To her left is another man that I immediately recognize. The father. His arm grasps the other two as if they have all become a single person. Then he sees me, and something like hope—ridiculous, remote hope—lights up his face. I want to say something, but what would it be? Sorry?

I don't even let my eyes betray that I recognize him. I keep walking. My officer signals to us.

"Hey, the freelancers stayed together," I say to him with a small laugh. "Isn't that something?" I try to laugh again. I feel sick. I do not look back.

✴ ✴ ✴

At the grocery store the next day, the cashier looks at my check. "Fire department, huh?" he says. "Great work schedule. Like, you don't work that much, right? Or you watch TV or something. Very cool."

I pay.

"Gosh, I'd like to have it that easy," he continues, not maliciously. He doesn't know any better. "Okay, well, right on, enjoy your day off and all that." He smiles at my good fortune, and turns to the next customer.

27.

Black smoke pumps heavily from the house when we arrive. The chief looks unhappy; the first arriving crews haven't found the seat of the fire yet, and the situation is devolving. Rescue 2 is only supposed to search and rescue, but today the chief growls, "Grab a line and find the goddamn thing." Frank sprints to a hose bed and dashes away with the nozzle, much to my dismay but not to my surprise. He's quicker and stronger than almost any of us.

Frank is new on the Rescue Squad. He's a young guy, with a military style crew cut, balloon sized muscles in his arms and shoulders, and a way of rocking back on his heels and jerking his head sideways to assess you before he speaks. His father is a chief and his uncle is a captain and his cousin is a firefighter and before that, his grandfather was a chief too. He's been visiting one firehouse or another since he was five years old. We become friends.

Frank likes to pretend he doesn't like the human race in general, but the truth is, I've only ever seen him be decent and polite. And in a fire, he's aggressive and smart. We usually try to pair up, but on this day we aren't partners, and I get Alberto, which is fine, but he's slow and this annoys me, especially at a fire. Now Frank charges into the garage, Andy behind him. I follow, with Victor trailing.

Inside, conditions seem pretty typical. Visibility is almost nil, and it's very, very hot. We're all crawling and dragging hose in that familiar, awkward conga line typical of every interior attack. We bump into walls and each other. There's shouting, but we can't make out what the other is saying. I wonder if Frank has any idea where he's going. Is the fire up ahead? I'm mid-thought, when the world explodes.

There is a great flash of light. There may have been noise, but I don't know. I don't know what happens next either, only that suddenly we are in the garage, untangling from each other. I sit up, dazed. Someone says, "Holy shit." Someone else says, "Flashover."

Then Frank is grabbing each of us by the shoulders and shouting, "Are you okay?! Are you okay?!" We are, it seems. Whatever room had flashed was far enough away to ensure our survival. Maybe it was an adjacent room and the walls saved us. Maybe a door was half-closed. It's only later that I process this. Ten seconds ahead, twenty more feet down the hallway, and we would have died.

In technical terms, flashovers happen "when the majority of surfaces in a space are heated to the autoignition temperature of the flammable gases, also known as Flash Point. Flashover normally occurs at 500 degrees Celsius (930 degrees Fahrenheit) or 1,100 degrees Fahrenheit for ordinary combustibles, and an incident heat flux at floor level of 1.8 Btu/foot."

But this is Wikipedia gibberish that hides the true horror, so let's put it in plain English.

A flashover is when the air explodes into flame.

Only a few seconds have passed and my brain isn't catching up to anything. I am simply a machine of surging chemicals, and the onslaught is making me shake. "Yes, I'm good," I manage to say to Frank. Andy pats his head and ears and curses. We're getting to our knees when Frank says, "Where's Victor?"

Victor? He isn't in the garage. Which means he's still inside. I process this in what seems like slow motion, then everything takes on a

surreal drawn-out quality. Frank, turning back slow as taffy toward the
interior door, Andy's curse words like a long, slow yawn in my ears.
Only I am not moving. Victor is my partner, therefore my responsibility. But suddenly I am frozen, stuck to the floor in some strange, para-
lyzed state I have never felt before.

And here is the thought, loud in my head and spoken in no uncertain terms: *I'm not going back in there.*

It takes only a second. But I hear the voice clearly. I squash it, quickly.
Then, as if fighting against a greater force in me, I clumsily follow
Frank, jamming on my air mask, sucking rapidly, forcing my arms and
legs to move, pinning my eyes to the smudged yellow reflector stripe
on his coat, pitching myself forward, knocking into his heels, back
through the doorway into the house. We find Victor within seconds;
he's unhurt, thankfully. When we had tumbled left, he had tumbled
right, taking cover in an adjoining room.

Back at the firehouse, we joke about the explosion, our burned
ears, the expression on the chief's face as we came somersaulting out
of the doorway into the garage. I want to tell Frank that he was a hell
of a brave guy back there, the first to think clearly, the first to act, but I
don't. I'm afraid if I do, it might lead to talk about what had happened
to me. And what had happened to me? I had been scared. Yet so had
Frank and Andy. But I had almost given in to that fear, and that was
what was scaring me most of all. Never in my whole firefighting life has
this come close to happening.

For the next few weeks, I tell myself over and over, *who cares that
I hesitated.* Within seconds, I was back in that hallway. But I have now
seen a part of myself I have not known about, that horrifies me.

I have been in many dangerous situations. I was once pulled into a
storm cloud while paragliding, a rare and stupid predicament cheerily
called "cloud sucked." It was scary, but I didn't freeze up. I executed a
series of emergency maneuvers to escape the cloud's interior updraft,

and succeeded (by the skin of my teeth). I once took a catamaran down a river that had only been rafted once before; my partner, a Russian who didn't speak English. In the middle of the most dangerous part of the rapid, he began to paddle left when I had been told that we had to paddle right. That was life threatening too, but no voice popped into my head telling me so, and my paddling arm didn't stop. After a few counter paddles, I decided to paddle with him, much to everyone's dismay on shore. We survived.

So why now? Why here? And what did it mean?

Months later, I begin to understand. I was lucky to have this moment. We all have a lurking coward in us; it's just a matter of when she shows. And now I have met her, and I know she's there, and I'm on guard. She's waiting for another scary moment, (and God knows there are many in this job) and then she'll raise her head, wave, beckon me over, and I'll be ready. I'll look her straight in the (proverbial) eye and say no, not you, not today.

28.

The phone wakes me at 8:00 A.M. I pat the bed, but Melea is already gone. I've slept late. I get up, thick with sleep, and pick up the receiver.

"Caroline. It's Kim." I am surprised to hear from her. As a police officer on the night shift, she should be sleeping now. Kim often swings her police car through my neighborhood and quietly checks on my house. Like many police officers, she is certain that the world is a grim and terrible place, and that her friends need to be constantly protected.

"Are you okay?" she asks.

"I just woke up," I say, thinking that perhaps my voice sounds slow and flu-like.

"No. I mean, you're okay, right?" There is something odd in her voice.

"Yes, sure." Kim is always protective, but this sounds different. "What do you mean?" The cat I have disturbed winds around my legs. I lean down and run my hand over her fur absently.

"Caroline, there was a big fire last night." Kim pauses, but already, instinctively, I know what she is going to say. I lean against the door. "Some firefighters were killed. One of them was a woman. I thought it might be you. Thank god it isn't."

❋ ❋ ❋

It had been a stormy night. In fact, it had been the brutal kind of storm that reminds us city dwellers that San Francisco is still a port town, subject to the furies of the ocean. The rain fell hard and copiously. The wind howled at up to 60 miles per hour. Trees shed branches and leaves under the onslaught, and visibility was terrible.

Probationer Cristine Prentice was sent to Station 50. She was teased about the detail; Station 50 is a sleepy station. It sits high on a hill with a beautiful view of downtown, Noe Valley, the Mission district, and the Bay Bridge. The common joke is that Station 50 will see every fire in the city, even if they never go to any of them. Engine 50, with probationer Cristine Prentice, rookie Gavin Wong and Lieutenant Thomas Shore, a veteran of 26 years, arrived alone.

The call for an activated residential smoke alarm came in at one o'clock in the morning. The alarm monitoring company that called the Fire Department Communications Center failed to indicate that this was a confirmed fire. As a result, the Communications Center dispatched it as a "2-1 box," which means that a full box, or a full first alarm contingent, are judged unnecessary. Engine 50, with probationer, Cristine Prentice, rookie, Gavin Wong and Lieutenant Thomas Shore, a veteran of 26 years, arrived alone.

The house is set into the hill to maximize the views. The garage is flush with the sidewalk; the rest of the house extends down behind the hill. This is a common design for Bay Area homes, and there seemed nothing unusual, not even smoke, when they pulled up. The owner was backing his Jaguar out of the garage. He said the fire, which had started at an outdoor electrical outlet, had been blown inside. Attempts to extinguish it had failed, so the family had dialed 911 soon after their alarm company had called. Shore radioed in a "working fire." A full box contingent would soon be on the way.

Conditions changed dramatically as the crew walked into the house. What was at first a small fire quickly became a large one because the shape of the house acted like a chimney for the high winds that night. As conditions worsened, Shore sent Wong back outside to help pump operator Dan Beckwith. Wong followed the hose through the now thick smoke, crawling through the blackness, and suddenly hit a solid wall. The hose was still in his hands; what could be the problem? Just moments before, the hose had led outside and to the engine. Now, the unthinkable had happened.

The garage door had closed.

Meanwhile, Truck 72 was at a call for a wire down just a few blocks away. The storm was wreaking havoc with the streets, but Truck 72 could find no problem wire there. Just then, the call for a full box went over the radio. Because Truck 72 had been dispatched on this "wire down" call, they were not called to the fire, though they would have been otherwise. Nick was the temporary lieutenant today, and he grabbed the radio phone. Like all firefighters, Truck 72 wanted to go to a fire, and besides, they were only a few blocks away. However, the dispatch center does not take kindly to requests to change initial dispatches. They don't want rogue crews intervening where they shouldn't. This is understandable; crews might leave medical or other scenes early in order to get in to a fire. Truck 72 was curtly told that they were not dispatched to the fire. Nick and his crew drove to the fire anyway.

There was no truck when they arrived. They noticed nothing wrong with Engine 50. Pump operator Beckwith was at the pump control panel, which was faced away from the garage. Beckwith could not see the disaster that had just happened.

From here on, the stories get confusing. Someone said he heard what he thought were cries for help, and later he will say, with his head in his hand, that he knows that it was Cristine's voice. Someone else said that Gavin Wong's hand was sticking out of a grate he had kicked out. Everybody said that the smoke was so heavy around the garage that you could not see the door.

Someone began yelling that there was a crew inside. People rushed at the door with axes. The smoke was so thick they could only take a few swings before retreating for air. Then they would lunge back in. From the roof, Nick saw a truckie from 72 start a large circular saw and walk straight into the smoke. This was a forbidden, dangerous move and Nick was stunned. Only then did he realize that Engine 50 was down, inside.

They got the door open. Two turnout coats were barely visible on the right side, another one on the left. There is nothing so terrible, Nick later told me, than seeing a firefighter down. "Those black and yellow coats, man, motionless. Just motionless," he said. In heavy smoke and fire, the crews dragged out Shore, Wong and Cristine.

Here was Nick's personal nightmare—*burns, man*—right in front of him. Shore, his face badly burned, was still. He did not respond at all. John Fisher, who was working that night, initiated CPR and stayed with it all the way to the hospital, even though he knew that Shore had died in the garage. You just don't give up, if it is a firefighter. You hold on, ridiculously, to hope. You keep doing CPR until they pull you off.

Cristine and Gavin were both responsive. Gavin walked around in a small circle, dazed. Cristine, initially unconscious, waved off help. "Take care of the others," she said. "I'm fine." But Nick, a paramedic, saw immediately that she was badly burned and in imminent respiratory danger. She had inhaled superheated gases and seared her lungs.

"She is *not* fine," Nick yelled. "Get her to the hospital NOW."

On a video that a civilian filmed, I see Nick pulling the gurney with Cristine on it. He has a determined look on his face; his large eyes look enormous. His helmet is off and his hair is plastered to his forehead. The rain is torrential. The wind is so high that people lean far forward as they run, straining against an invisible force. The trees whip around frantically; embers are flying everywhere. Later, someone who had been in Vietnam said that the fire was the worst thing he had ever seen. Worse than a strafing, he said.

Sharks and burns. Firefighters down. A nightmare come true.

✵ ✵ ✵

I call Station 64 immediately. They tell me the news: Cristine is in critical condition and she is not expected to live. Lt. Thomas Shore is dead. Gavin Wong, though burned on his hands and neck, will survive.

I begin to cry. It's a flood of grief that makes me wonder who I am really crying for, them or myself.

I wonder if Cristine regretted it, being a firefighter. Maybe a little, just at the moment when the heat overtook them.

Cristine is not only another woman, she is a probationer at my station. Though I did not know her well, the fire department has taught me about inherent loyalties. A few years ago, I would have kept my grief to myself. But I have learned much since then.

Still, I do not know what to do. Firefighters are being told not to go to the hospital. Otherwise, it would be packed. For all I know, Cristine has already died. I take a few deep breaths and pick up the phone. There is one person to call, one person who would know what to do.

Patricia answers cheerily. I am determined not to cry on the phone—Patricia is the last person I want to cry in front of—but I can only get out a *hello, Patricia?* before I have to stop. She clearly has not heard about the fire yet.

"Go to the hospital," she says. She did not know Wong or Cristine, but she knows Lt. Shore. "A real gentleman," she murmurs. "Go to the hospital," she says again. "Who the fuck cares that they said not to? This is about another firefighter."

Patricia is right, once again.

A small waiting room has been set up. The food spread out by the Local is untouched but coffee flows freely. Everyone looks terrible. People hug or touch elbows.

Joe McGinnis, of the Union, walks up to me. He is a handsome man with exuberant gestures. Even now his energy is uncontainable, though his eyes are red and swollen. He shakes my hand in wide, earnest arcs.

"We need to contact Cristine's friends, her family. We know she has a sister in Connecticut and there is a brother on the way." He lowers his voice. "But does she have a, you know, girlfriend, we should call?" He stares at me earnestly. "This whole thing is unbelievable, with Tommie and..." His voice trails off. He blinks.

Jonathan Hunt is here, and he makes his way quickly to me.

"It doesn't look good," he says of Cristine. "Second degree burns and some third degree over 50 percent of her body. The second degree can still revert to third—it is all still burning in there. The lungs are the big problem. They took x-rays. Good lungs are black and bad lungs come up gray. About 20 percent of her lungs are white."

Stories are flying around now, competing versions of the same incident. They weren't wearing air packs. They were, but they didn't use them. Wong lived because he turned his air pack down to save air. (This last statement is overtly false. The new air packs do not have a regulatory valve, though the old ones did.) Cristine Prentice pulled her mask off in a panic before her air was out. The owner in the Jaguar closed the garage door by accident. The fire shorted the wires out, and the garage door closed. The firefighters leaned on the inside button as they entered the house; they closed the door unwittingly and sealed their fate.

There is no way to know the true story yet. Gavin and Cristine are unconscious. Thomas Shore is dead. A full investigation will happen later. Still, there is something comforting in trying to make sense of it all. *There*, we could say. *That's why.*

The intensive care staff is patient with the growing crowd in the halls. Firefighters keep showing up. The long vigil begins.

At Station 50, there is already a black wreath on the door. The flag is at half mast. A television crew pulls up as I get out of the car. The camera operator aims his camera at the station. He zooms in on the wreath. Another man primps in the side mirror of the television van, ready to translate this tragedy into catchy sound bites.

The communications room mills with firefighters, both on- and off-duty. The phone rings incessantly. One firefighter blinks hard as he greets me, but the captain of the station lets tears stream down his face unchecked. He hugs me and asks about Cristine, wiping his face with one hand.

"It looks bad," I say. "She's been given last rites." This is true; the department chaplain, fearing her imminent death, has administered them by the hospital bed. Unfortunately, Cristine is not Catholic. This last minute conversion might strike her as funny, and in my hopeful mind, I imagine her waking up, coming back to the firehouse and turning her newfound religious conversion into a Fire Story. But she might also be baffled that she was surrendered so easily, when she herself was not yet giving up.

I've come here for Cristine's belongings, so I walk reluctantly into the dorm. Her gear bag is in the corner, as if she will come back any minute and pack it up. Her sleeping bag is pushed aside, and I imagine that she was quick to get out of her bunk and into her turnout gear. She was an eager, earnest probationer, and this was her dream job.

She's not dead yet, but it still feels strange to pack her stuff. I'm not just packing items, I'm packing her intention to live. *She dropped her clothes in a pile here*, I think to myself, *because she thought she was returning to fold them. She placed her toothbrush here, and her dental floss there because she was supposed to come back to use it. She left her book open to that page, because she thought she was going to finish reading it.*

As I pass through the apparatus floor, I catch sight of three pairs of dirty, wet turnout gear strewn on the floor. Air packs are nearby. I turn my head away. I have caught a glimpse of ghosts, and I do not want to see anymore. As I leave, more television vans pull up.

Cristine does not die the first day. On the second day, the intensive care staff allows firefighters to enter two at a time and stand at the glass windows of each of the rooms. I decline. Only by mid-afternoon, when about twelve female firefighters have gathered, do I decide to go in. We ask for a few minutes with Cristine. The head nurse nods. "Only a few minutes, though," she adds. She is large and imposing. We assure her that's all we need.

We stand at the glass. Nothing could prepare us for this sight. Cristine is heavily bandaged. Her face is grotesquely swollen and bright red and shiny, as if just polished. She is hooked up to an immense number of tubes and machines. They blink and squirm monotonously. I try to interpret the meaning of the numbers, but my rudimentary medical skills are not up to it. All of us are crying, and we're not ashamed of it. Otherwise we say nothing. What is there to say? Even Amy, never at a loss for words, is silent. Behind us is Gavin's intensive care room, but curtains are drawn over the glass. As we turn to leave, each one of us stops momentarily in front.

Cristine's mother is almost seventy. She has flown in from Hawaii and has the exhausted, drawn expression any parent would have at this moment. She is accompanied by Cristine's best friend who has extremely short, dyed hair and a ring through her lower lip. More of Cristine's friends arrive. Their hair is also dyed in various colors and they wear rings through their noses or lips. It is a strange scene: uniformed personnel dispersed among orange-haired, multi-tattooed, pierced women and men. Two sub-cultures, vastly different, meeting and mingling. *Only in the fire department*, I think, as I watch a large male firefighter nod and extend a hand to a petite woman with a ring through her nose and a mermaid tattooed on her forearm.

I tell my family. My father inhales sharply, and I know he has gone pale on the other end of the phone. He is silent, just as he was when I first told him about the fire department. This time, he does not think about "phases." He thinks about losing his daughter, but he does not say this. He says "be careful" before we hang up but he does not mention today, as he usually does, that I give him all the gray hairs that he has. Today it would not be funny. It would be too close to the truth.

Cris has made it through the first thirty-six hours. This is a miracle, though the head doctor pulls me aside and shakes his head. "We are not telling the family this," he says. "But it won't be long now."

At this moment someone else from Truck 72 pushes out of the intensive care doors. He wipes his eyes. "I just stood there, and stood there," he murmurs, shaking his head. "Tears running down my face like crazy."

The funeral for Thomas Shore is held in a large white church, with a marble entrance half a city block long. Here most of the off-duty department gathers, boots finely polished and dress jackets pressed. It is raining hard, so people mill around the sprawling staircase, or snap umbrellas shut and walk into the church. When the wind picks up, I am reminded of the storm that started all this. I am an usher today; Amy and I will seat Shore family friends. White gloves are passed around, and emergency workers begin to walk into the rain to line up in long, dark rows. There are thousands, many from other fire departments around the state. Police officers have come, because Lt. Shore's son is a police officer, but there are also highway patrol personnel, sheriffs, paramedics and retired city workers. The expanse in front of the church is now almost full, the dark rows of personnel striping the marble like a flag.

I wave and nod to the people I know—almost everyone from the San Francisco Fire Department. *Six years*, I think. Even those I only recognize murmur greetings.

Coulda been me, our minds whisper. A different shift, a different station, a different detail. Each of us calculates the distance between ourselves and that fateful day. For some, the distance is small. For me, it was a shift away. In fact, next shift I am up for the detail, though I do not know it yet, and I will be sent to Station 50. *Oooh*, fellow firefighters will tease, *the bad luck detail from Station 64*, and I will laugh too. For others, especially the two firefighters at 50 who were replaced by Gavin and Cris, that fateful day was very close indeed.

"Hey," someone says. It is Ritch, from my academy class, his long hand lightly on my elbow, nodding slowly. His cap is slightly off kilter. It makes him look young.

"Good to see you," he says.

His narrow blue eyes are expressionless. He pauses and I know what we are both thinking. *Glad you didn't eat it, kick the can, bite the big one, blow the pop top, crash and burn, terminate, deactivate...*

"How's Rescue 2?" he asks.

... Amp out, lose the lolly, bite it, catch the crispy ...

"Good, good. It's home now." ... *DOA, rigor out, decease, pass on ...*

"We're getting on, that's for sure."

... pass away...

"Yup. Shoot. It's been six years."

... die.

I watch him walk away. He had promised once that it would be simple. *Little fire, little hose. Big fire, big hose.* But it has never been that easy.

I watch Thomas, who has always looked out for me, shake rain from his sleeve. Then there is Chief Kalafferty, who, without hesitation, bent every department rule on the strength of my word. Across the pew, Chief Masters waves. He looks tired. He goes to the hospital every shift to bring food to the Prentice family and friends. Other firefighters, too, arrive with food, their crisp, straight creases and belted pants incongruous against the loose leather jackets and baggy jeans of Cristine's friends.

I like to see Masters walking into a room of Cristine's friends. He introduces himself to everyone and stays to make conversation. I am once more impressed and intrigued by the San Francisco firemen.

As the casket is lifted from the back of Engine 50, a bell, signaling the final alarm of Lt. Thomas Shore, is tolled. The resonance of each ring rolls over us for a long time, while we hold a salute. The rain continues.

The casket comes slowly up the marble. There's a fire helmet on top. The pallbearers are tight faced and pale. Some cry openly.

The service is short and somber. The church, the largest I have ever seen, is overflowing with mourners.

At this moment, Engine 50's pump operator is on the other side of the city. He is found stumbling around in the rain, crying, at the scene of the fire. The house is now silent, girded with yellow police tape. Flowers lie at the garage door.

At the end of the service, the firefighters and police officers file out. Amy and I follow, taking our places once more in the long, straight rows. The color guard calls out a command and a salute, thousands of hands long, snaps to attention. The coffin makes its slow way back to Engine 50 as taps are played.

Now the long, thin cry of the siren begins. It is the sound we hear every day, as familiar to us as a telephone ring to a business executive. It never fails to raise the hair at the back of my neck, to race my heart. Today, I get the chill again, but there is a mixture of melancholy and apprehension.

People ask me if I still want to do this work. The answer is, *of course*. We go into this career knowing that death and injury are inherent possibilities. Today is heartbreaking, but not a surprise.

An old-timer said to me once, years ago, it seems, "You gotta be scared of fire. Anyone tells you they ain't scared of fire, they're either lying or they've never really been in a good one. Gotta be scared by it, because then you'll respect it. Then, you'll live to fuck your wife— excuse me—sleep with your wife, play with the kids, smell the flowers, as they say." This is fire's most important lesson.

The casket is lifted and laid in the hose bed. The siren continues. Even when we drop our salute—two thousand swishes of wool sleeves slapped against thighs—no one moves.

The procession is hundreds of rigs long. It travels slowly—this is the way grief moves. People stop on the sidewalk, pushing their umbrellas back to look. Homeless people emerge from behind swad-dled shopping carts. If they are military vets, they snap to a perfect salute and stand that way until the whole procession passes. Mothers lean to their children, whispering. The children stare, chewing on their hands, wide-eyed.

A firefighter died, they will say. *In a big, bad fire. See, sweetheart, all the lights? A firefighter died and this is a very sad day.*

Police and parking control officers stop traffic, and then swivel around to pay their respects. In their cars, people turn down their radios, open their windows. The procession is silent, a long line of flashing lights, but I imagine I hear the slow, insistent wail of Engine 50. As they make their way to the burial ground, fire engines wait at each overpass and footbridge. The casket passes underneath, and each new engine crew responds overhead with a long, silent salute. The emergency beacons glint like halos, with the slow, solemn pulse of a last alarm.

29.

Our first call of the day is for a person with AIDS over on Mariposa Street. There is nothing we can do for him but put an oxygen mask onto his face. It starts to rain.

That's the sort of place you gotta breathe shallow in, ya know?, someone once said, back when AIDS was still a fairly new phenomenon. He had washed his hands as soon as he got back to the station, changed his shirt and shaken out his turnout coat. "They say you can't get it by being close," he had added, "But they all lie. All of them. You just can't be too careful."

Things have changed now—there is less fear, and more awareness. There is also more protection for the firefighter—gloves, masks and adequate information. AIDS has hit San Francisco hard, and it's not just the gay population. This disease is open to everyone: straights and non-drug-users, too. I have seen a sixty-year-old grandmother with AIDS; all we could do was put an oxygen mask on her as well.

Now I want to wash this morning's image out of my mind, the image of that drawn, wasted body, with the skin that looks like crackly paper. The mother, gray-haired and bulbous, had put her hand lightly on my arm. She'd handed me my helmet, tried to say something, then had leaned into my shoulder and cried.

I think of Mrs. Prentice, standing vigil over her daughter. Cris is still in the hospital. She has survived the critical forty-eight-hour window. Since then, she has also survived pneumonia, pancreatitis, lung collapse, and burn infection. Before work this morning, I stop by the emergency room to check on Cris's mother and her friends who keep 24-hour-vigil. They talk, sing, and laugh to her. They rub her feet and hands. They play her favorite music, from Al Green to Johnny Cash. The intensive care staff encourage this—all part of the healing process, they say. If you watch through the glass, you can see Mrs. Prentice nodding to Cash's "A Boy Named Sue". When I walk into the small room that the hospital has given the family to sleep in, I startle Cris's mother. She thinks I am a nurse arriving with bad news. She sits up from the sofa, disheveled from the night before. She greets me with a smile, then puts her head in her hands and weeps. No mother should endure this, I think.

I arrive back at the station and head for the coffee pot with a nod at Alan. Paul pats the sofa beside him and I sit down, holding the coffee I will hardly touch.

Today I will drive, because Miller is not here. I remember that it is Joe's day off as well. I wonder who our officer will be. I sit down at a table and glance at the Rescue officer's desk. I almost choke on my small sip of coffee.

Todd Lane stands there. I have only seen him three times since I left Station 4, and that was at fires where I could duck my chin into my collar and slide behind a rig. If I could not avoid him, I turned my head away, without a word. But I would recognize him anywhere. He is stamped indelibly in my mind.

"Who's the Squad boss today?" I ask Paul. Paul is on the engine so he is not likely to know. I want to ask Alan but I do not want him to see that I am bothered. He knows about the trouble with Todd Lane; he was there that day. As a probationer, all he could do was watch in silence, but later he told me *that was bullshit* and shook his head.

"Lane, I think," Paul now says.

"Uh huh," I say, as casually as possible.

Lane looks up from the desk. He walks towards the kitchen, frowning. He holds the list of today's Squad members in his hand. I know that he is trying to figure out who his driver and his emergency medical technician for the day will be. I should be driving, but this would mean that I would spend the whole day in the cab, with him sitting next to me. This seems unthinkable, to have only a gearshift between me and the person who has, for all these years, symbolized to me the narrow-mindedness and fear of this institution. On the other hand, why should I let Todd Lane run my life? I want to drive. If I do not drive because he is there, then he wins.

Forget it. I'm not going to drive. I want to be as far away from him as possible. My stomach feels tight and my throat is dry, even after all these years. Alan can drive and I will be in the back as the EMT, a thick wall of steel and noise between us. Todd Lane is a loutish, malicious person.

Lane stops at the head of the table. He looks the same: heavy-jowled and small-eyed.

"Who's on the Squad?" he asks. Alan waves in response.

"I am, too." I say. Lane looks back with a slight quizzical air. He hesitates, and then says, "And you are … ?"

He does not know my name. Momentarily, this astounds me. I have affixed his every mean feature in my head, would recognize his every arrogant gesture from one hundred yards away. There is only one incident between us, and I cannot even repeat it to people without a profound physiological change coming over me. I feel myself become pale, and the prickly beginnings of sweat start at my collar. My voice becomes tight and my eyes go flat. The incident is vivid in my mind, and the emotions associated with it remain etched in my psyche. He has affected the way I interact with the department. But he does not even remember who I am.

"I'm the driver today," I say.

Today's rain falls in a small, grim spray that makes the hot May morning seem heavier and hotter. Soon, it stops. The sky breaks blue. I wrestle with whether to talk to Lane at all; maybe I will just maintain a stony silence. Let him be uncomfortable for a while. I practice various versions of *okay, asshole, why were you so hateful four years ago?*

I have been taught that politeness is next to godliness, and I decide that I will suffer more than he from a stony silence. I settle for a tone that is businesslike and sentences that are short and to the point. But I will not succumb into the almost irresistible urge to be "nice," to the need to be liked. Todd Lane will not play on my insecurities a second time.

"We need batteries for a flashlight, and we can go without gas for the rig today," is all I tell him.

The morning is quiet, and we head into the afternoon with no calls at all. This is highly unusual for Rescue 2, especially on a hot day. Fate, God or Lady Luck all seem to agree: no sense in my having to be in the cab with Todd Lane.

At the kitchen table, a listless game of Pedro is played. I enjoy watching the men play cards; they hold their cards softly and jealously, throw barbed glances at each other, tease and joke. Between hands, there is talk of the latest diet bet going on. Who can lose twenty pounds in a month? In the final week, participants start to panic. They cut out liquor. They jog in layers of heavy clothing around the station house. The ones who were smart enough to weigh in with five large eight-ounce glasses of water in them and a full bladder try to think up new tricks. If someone on your shift is in on the diet bet, you cook his favorite meal that night and snicker while he watches everyone eat it from behind his glass of Slim Fast.

Finally, at five-thirty in the afternoon, a call comes in. It is a shooting at the housing projects. Luckily, there is no time to talk as we dodge and duck in and out of afternoon traffic, sirens and air horn blaring. When the patient has been "packaged," extra hands are needed in the ambulance to help the paramedics on the way to the hospital. Lane and I will follow in the rig.

"That is where my old high school was," Lane says, pointing. I nod and let out a sound in my throat that I hope is acknowledgement, but not interest. "Sure was a long time ago," he adds. He seems to be trying to be pleasant, but then again, I will not be a fool. Luckily, there is little more to say, because we are at the hospital. Alan and Riley hop on and we head back to Station 64, which is only five minutes or so away.

The full box comes in within half an hour. *Many phone calls*, the dispatcher adds, and we know that it will be good. Big. And we are right; we see the smoke rising from the bottom of the hill, still ten blocks away. We already know what the first engine to arrive radios in: "Working fire," and "Give us a second alarm!"

The paint factory is "fully involved" when we pull up; large billows of smoke belch from the roof and flames have already broken through. Lane is not used to the gear of a Squad, and I notice with satisfaction that he has entangled himself in the officer's belt and not yet thrown on his air pack. I won't wait for him; I enter the warehouse next to the paint factory. The wide, roll-up doors have been flung open and inside it is head-high with cardboard boxes. With an axe in one hand and a nozzle in the other, I clamber up the stacks and towards the lath and plaster wall. If we get through the wall, we can get water on the fire and, we hope, advance to its seat.

I begin to chop at the lath and plaster, cradling the nozzle between my knees. It is awkward, but it works. The wall shears off easily, revealing metal corrugation underneath. I swing at the metal, but someone yells my name. Todd Lane stands there with a chainsaw.

He is known for his work with a chainsaw, as someone else might be known for facility with a gun. Sure enough, he is confident and precise and the corrugation sags with each quick cut. I stand to one side, ready with the nozzle in case of fire right behind the wall. It is not lost on me, this sudden camaraderie. Lane may not think a woman can do this job, but he knows that if there is fire behind the wall, I am the one he must rely on.

A third alarm is pulled and the roof begins to collapse. The loud sounds of exploding paint rat-tats the air. By now we have moved deeper into the warehouse, chopping holes in the corrugation and sending streams of water in. Todd Lane is nearby, but I doubt he even notices me. We know the paint factory is lost. Our goal is to contain the fire now and to save the warehouse and the residences on the south side.

More paint explodes nearby. Everyone ducks.

Thick, black smoke shrouds the nearby freeway. Traffic comes to a standstill. Long, white rivers of paint stream down the streets. A fourth alarm is pulled.

The rest of the fire goes like this: chop holes, find a hose line, aim it into the paint factory. It vents easily: all the visibility issues are now from the steam of the master streams that rain down from the aerial ladders. The flames persist. As firefighters say to describe a good greater alarm, "There is enough fire for everyone."

I squat by a hole I have made with the large, powerful circular saw. There's not much to see because of the steam, but I can hear. Fire like this sounds like an oncoming train. The building creaks and groans and cracks. Every so often, more paint explodes, sending what looks like fireworks into the air. Timbers give way with muffled thumps, and the metal corrugation whines as it bends. Every so often, too, the air will clear slightly and I will make out the gangly remains of the structure. It is defeated now, splayed out and tired.

I have left my air pack far behind, but I remember the respirator in my pocket. It helps some, and when the roof is mostly collapsed, it allows me to crawl into the factory with a hose. Even with the respirator, however, I can feel that toxic edge to the fumes. Tomorrow, health officials will assure the public that there was nothing dangerous in the air, no need to worry about airborne contaminants. I know different: my throat stings and my eyes feel swollen and sore. Every so often, I cannot breathe at all.

The paint keeps exploding, but now with less vigor. A hard space inside me, heavy and sealed like the paint cans, splits and begins to leak away. I stay perched in my peculiar doorway, which is badly cut because I do not have the tool skills that Lane has. I watch the remains of the building heave and sigh. A crew from Station 27 wanders by. They pick up hose and kick through the ankle-deep water to check for sunken equipment—axes, ceiling hooks, air packs. Patricia is their pump operator today—she is four blocks away at a hydrant. From her vantage point, all she will see is the smoke rise and change color according to whether her colleagues are winning or losing the battle. She will be fretful that she can only watch. "Tell her she missed a good one," I tell her crew, knowing that my remark will further infuriate her. The thought makes me smile.

The stricken warehouse collapses slowly and with a kind of outraged dignity—first the inside in bits and pieces, jerkily and unwilling, and then the outside with a huge crash. It had started out a bad day, but now I feel better. My crew had been first in on the west side, and I was on the nozzle—you couldn't beat that. Even Todd Lane can't take this away.

There is nothing more to do except make my way to the front and reconnect with my crew. Lane is already there, making one last hole in a wall. I steady the metal for him while he cuts. Paint streams from the factory, thick and white. This fire will smolder for a long time, and crews will be posted on "fire watch" all night and into the next day. For now, there is nothing more that the Squad can do. Lane and I straighten up and stare at the factory, now only a vast space full of debris. Darkened, splintered posts hint of the structure it was. The building beside it is intact except for the many holes gnawed out of one side. Behind, the two-story homes that abutted the factory have long black streaks of fire damage down their sides. But they remain standing.

"Good job," says Lane, nodding my way.

Perhaps it is the adrenalin still kinked inside the interstitial places. Perhaps fire simply wipes away small cautions. Or is it the sheer joy of watching something so huge and powerful leap so close, like a beautiful animal in the wild? Whatever the reason, I turn to him and look him straight in the eye.

"You're joking, right?" I say. I shake my head, stammering out a laugh, feeling strangely delighted. "After all, you hate me. You once told everyone you wanted to make my life miserable, and in your small way, you did."

He looks shocked. There is a pause, and then slowly recognition hits. Before he can respond, Masters walks up. "Squad, go home," he says nodding at the both of us. "And great job."

In the cab of the rig, Lane clears his throat.

"You know," he says. He looks at the dashboard. He speaks slowly. "I'm not excusing what I may have done, but, women coming in, it was hard."

I stare straight ahead.

"This might sound odd," he continues, "but the fire department was the best men's club in the world. And then women came in and it all changed. It wasn't easy." He pauses.

"But I'm different now. I've changed. You've got to change—more women are in and they're going to keep coming in. I see men who refuse to change, who hang on and they are bitter and it's killing them, eating them up. I'm different now."

Why should I listen to him? He sounds sincere, but he may go back to Station 4 and laugh. *Remember that girl*, he will say, *that girl—what's her name?* And he will tell the whole story as if I am an idiot.

"I think I get along pretty well with some of the women." He sounds slightly confused. "Maybe some of the old-time women, the women who first got in, they hate me, but what can you do. I have a son now. He's two years old. And women come up to me and say, hey Todd, how's your son?"

I flick the emergency lights on and veer left across the street to back into the station. Once in, I cut the engine. Todd doesn't make a move to leave.

"I'm not like I was. I'm not proud of everything I've done." He shrugs and frowns through the windshield.

There's another pause. It's gotten uncomfortable but it seems we both want some closure. I check myself. I'm not angry. I'm just tired.

I say, "Okay, I believe you." And then add, "I appreciate you telling me."

Without another word, we exit the cab. I begin to take off the dirty tools and switch the tanks on the air packs.

Alan walks up. You can't get much by him.

"Everything okay?" he asks, turning on a hose to help me clean the equipment, which smells sour with paint and ash.

"You won't believe what happened," I say. And I tell him.

Alan shakes his head. "And you trust him? People don't just change like that," he says.

"You know, I think I do believe him. I can't say why, exactly, but I do."

We go back to wiping off tools and air packs, and hosing our boots down.

An hour and a half later, the other crews start drifting back. There is much milling around, tellings and retellings of the fire. Everyone's skin is streaked with black ash and white paint. Suddenly, from the Rescue desk, Todd Lane beckons me over.

He hitches his pants and clears his throat. "Listen," he says, his voice low. "Is it too late, four years too late, to say I'm sorry?"

Funny, you wait for a moment for years, and then there it is and you can't think of anything to say, and worse, you can't even summon up the kind of satisfaction you thought you would feel. Instead, I feel only relief, and something else, an inner quietness perhaps. I watch as Lane walks away, wiping paint and ash off his hair.

EPILOGUE

I take the line out of the firefighter's hands as he crouches on the sidewalk, too far from the building, really, for an aggressive attack. He doesn't have gloves on. I point this out to him and then reach for the nozzle, as if doing him a favor.

"Put on your gloves," I hiss. I act astonished at this breach of safety, and then snatch the nozzle and drag the hose toward the stairwell. Right inside the doorway, it becomes dark almost immediately, except for an orange glow above. I have time to think how beautiful it is before some of the roof falls in and knocks me and my newly-gloved partner back momentarily. But we move quickly up the stairs after this, spraying into the eerie luminescence unique to a good, hot fire.

Someone is yelling to back out, but I feel fine; I already know how I will bail out if more hell breaks loose. The stairwell banister is to my right and it will not be so bad a fall. The air is hot and I guess that just a few feet above me it has reached about one thousand degrees, so I lie down completely flat, which is when I feel the burn on both shins. Embers perhaps. Or steam from the hot water.

I don't know who is behind me. Whoever they are, they're doing a good job relieving the weight of the hose. In front of me, it sounds as if a giant rock slide is beginning. The room glows. The water falls back in rumbles and roars. The heat is suffocating.

And I can't help it: I feel happy.

Later, I find out that the fire got around us, and behind. Someone from Station 64 falls through the roof. He hangs there while truckies scramble to grab him. I do not see any of this and later when he tells the story, he acts as if it's nothing. He laughs that his large belly stopped his fall. "Food saved my life," he says. We laugh too, but we know that he's lucky. We're all lucky.

Cris is out of her coma. Despite terrible odds, she is alive. But she is blind. She shouldn't even have lived, the doctors say. It is a miracle. The burns up her legs are bad, though in time, they will heal. Her eyes will not. She goes from the darkness of the garage to the darkness of a coma and now to a new darkness. Crazily enough, all she wants is to be a firefighter again. This seems impossible, but who knows. She's tough. She has beaten all the odds before.

She hangs out with two retired firefighters. They entered the San Francisco Fire Department just after World War II, almost fifty years ago, back when it was unthinkable that a woman could do the job. Cris's friends have drifted away, as friends do when the drama of tragedy is over and the monotony of tragedy begins, but these retired firefighters are different. They call her every few days. "Hey Cris, hiya," they say. "Let's have dinner tomorrow." Other times, they take her for walks. They go slowly, because her legs are still wrapped in bandages, and I have seen them put their arms out protectively when they think that she might fall. It does not matter to them that Cris is a woman. She is a firefighter. To them, she is a member of their own big-armed, chain-smoking, hard-drinking crew.

The firefighters at Lt. Shore's station finished work on a house for his wife. It was a house in the country that Lt. Shore had started to build, and had planned to retire to.

Station 4 raised one thousand dollars for Cris.

Life goes on here at Station 64. The largest station in San Francisco, it is a good mix of men, women, blacks, whites Asians, Hispanics, and other. The endless cycle of life, death, and birth continues in the Mission District, and everywhere else.

The fire triangle has finally been changed to the fire tetrahedron, or so I saw in a recent fire magazine.

The San Francisco Fire Department has its first black chief, appointed by the city's first black mayor.

San Francisco's Department of Public Health will soon merge into the fire department. This means that ambulances will be stationed in firehouses and that paramedic work will become part of the fire department. A lot of firefighters are unhappy about this, including me. *What about fires?* We moan. *What about the good old days?*

Change is hard, after all.

There is talk of closing down some firehouses altogether. Money, as usual. Hopefully, San Franciscans won't allow it. It's like canceling the insurance policy. Everyone says, *it won't happen to me.* And then it does, and each minute counts.

Alexandra will soon leave *Baywatch*. She likes her work there, but her agents tell her it is time to move on. The producers want to marry her character off, but she insists on death during a rescue and poignant last words. Jonathan moves on, too, to Oregon. He is deep in the backcountry, living near both Earth First environmentalists and radical white separatists. He is happy, powering his life with solar panels and hydropower from a nearby creek. He organizes anti-logging demonstrations.

My mother and I talk every couple weeks or so. I like it when she visits. We are making up for lost time.

My father calls every other day. He tells me again that I gave him all his gray hairs. I tell him that Alexandra and Jonathan deserve equal credit.

The burn is not so bad, just blisters that rise and then wither in a few weeks. There are worse burns. I stare at the dark patches and know that in some perverse way, I am glad for the way the moment has marked me. It is a moment when, in the dark and heat, life is finally precious. Finally, for me, it is truly and deeply felt.

As for this book, it began as a story of an institution and the people who changed it. But really, it is about the way the institution and its struggles changed me. But that is the way it is with a Fire Story. Everyone has one, and you never really know how it ends until you get there.

ACKNOWLEDGEMENTS

Thanks to Holly Payne, of Skywriter Books, for publishing this new edition. To Wendy MacNaughton, who stood by patiently while I fretted, and who talked through issues and chapters with me. To all of you at the Writer's Grotto, for the inspiration, guidance and friendship.

And for the original edition:
Thanks to my agent, Charlotte Sheedy, who would have made a formidable firefighter herself. Thanks also to Elaine Pfefferblit, my original editor, who had the burden of working with a first time writer, and did so with humor, patience and skill. And to Michael Denneny, who did the final edit.

To the readers of the original manuscript: Keith Abell, Erik Gaull, Elizabeth Leahy, Marni Hine, Katie Hubbard, Kay K., Gina Macintosh, Eric Martin, Stephen Muller, Ken Olsen (I owe you dinner), Jim Paul, and Beth Rypins—all of whom gave incisive critiques and an occasional white lie.

To Farley's Café, which let me use an electrical outlet and a corner table. To the Babar writers, especially Jim, who encouraged and advised me. To the Green family, who kept me asking all the wacky questions of life. To my family: Sarah Paul, Mark Paul, Alexandra and Jonathan, for their unflagging enthusiasm and their constant support. To the many firefighters who shared their stories and opinions. And to Trish Lee, who put up with it all.

Many of the firefighters and fire stations have been renamed, and some events have been compressed or chronologically rearranged. Because this book spans many years, and some of it has been rewritten only recently, much of the original dialogue has been forgotten. Spoken phrases are not exact quotes, but remain as true to the original circumstances as I remember. Some sentences are unforgettable, however; those are transcribed exactly as they were said.

ABOUT THE AUTHOR

Caroline Paul was a San Francisco firefighter from 1989 to 2003. She is the author of the historical novel, East Wind, Rain, and works out of the Writer's Grotto in San Francisco. When she's not writing, she flies experimental planes. More about Caroline can be found at http://www.carolinepaul.com

CPSIA information can be obtained at www.ICGtesting.com
Printed in the USA
BVOW032127161012

303168BV00001B/17/P